MIGHTY CASEY

Albert Dorne's painting of "Mighty Casey" striking out. Courtesy of John Hancock Mutual Life Insurance Company.

MIGHTY CASEY

All-American

EUGENE C. MURDOCK

Contributions to the Study of Popular Culture, Number 7

GREENWOOD PRESS
Westport, Connecticut · London, England

Library of Congress Cataloging in Publication Data

Murdock, Eugene Converse.
  Mighty Casey, all-American.

  (Contributions to the study of popular culture,
ISSN 0198-9871 ; no. 7)
  Bibliography: p.
  1. Thayer, Ernest Lawrence, 1863–1940. Casey at the
bat.   2. Thayer, Ernest Lawrence, 1863–1940—Parodies,
travesties, etc.   3. Baseball in literature.   4. Base-
ball—Poetry.   5. American poetry.   I. Title.
II. Series.
PS3014.T3C336   1984   811'.52   83-16338
ISBN 0-313-24075-2 (lib. bdg.)

Library of Congress Catalog Card Number: 83-16338
ISBN: 0-313-24075-2
ISSN: 0198-9871

First published in 1984

Greenwood Press
A division of Congressional Information Service, Inc.
88 Post Road West
Westport, Connecticut 06881

Printed in the United States of America

10 9 8 7 6 5 4 3 2 1

COPYRIGHT ACKNOWLEDGMENTS

Grateful acknowledgment is made to the following persons and publishers for permission to use their materials:

"Cool Casey at the Bat" © 1960 by E. C. Publications, Inc., and "Casey at the Dice" © 1968 by E. C. Publications, Inc., both of which appeared in *Mad*.

W. H. Schuman and Jeremy Gury, *The Mighty Casey*. Copyright © 1954 by G. Schirmer, Inc. All rights reserved. Used by permission.

Darrell Berrigan, "The Truth about Casey." Reprinted from *The Saturday Evening Post* © 1954 The Curtis Publishing Company.

Every reasonable effort has been made to trace the owners of copyright material in this book, but in some instances this has proven impossible. The publishers will be glad to receive information leading to more complete acknowledgment in subsequent printings of the book and in the meantime extend their apologies for any omissions.

Contents

viii   Contents

Illustrations

Preface

Putting this book together has been sheer fun. Along with many other Americans, baseball enthusiasts or not, I learned about "Casey at the Bat" at a rather early age, and it has remained part of my "intellectual" baggage across the years. I began reciting the poem probably in the early 1950s and started collecting variations on the theme sometime later. I had not accumulated very many, however, when Martin Gardner published his fascinating *Annotated Casey at the Bat* in 1967. To me this was just about the *ultimate* baseball book.

But as I read over old issues of *Sporting Life*, *The Sporting News*, and *Baseball Magazine*, I ran across a number of additional parodies of the poem. In time I had so many I thought I should do something with them. I decided to group them in logical categories, even though many inconsistencies within the categories cropped up. Basically, this collection occupies part two of the book.

As I became more familiar with the subject, I learned that there was a real dispute over the authorship of "Casey at the Bat," and a couple of tongue-in-cheek arguments about "Casey" and "Mudville." These were natural topics for historical analysis. The chapters devoted to such matters constitute the substance of part one.

I would like to express my appreciation to Martin Gardner, the pioneer "Casey" scholar, for his encouragement and support of this enterprise and for granting permission to use a great deal of material from *The Annotated Casey at the Bat*. I would also like to thank Charles Alexander of Ohio University, Tristram Coffin of the University of Pennsylvania, Tilden Edelstein of Rutgers, Harry Lupold of Lakeland Community College, and Paul Frisz of Terre Haute, Indiana, for bringing to my attention obscure "Casey" poems and clearing up puzzles in the "Casey" story. Among those who made my job a bit easier were the librarians at Marietta College, Bernice Barry, Sandra Neyman, and Phyllis Zoerkler. In addition, my thanks to the editors and staff of Greenwood Press, Dr. James Sabin, Halley Gatenby, and Judith Lola, for putting the manuscript in proper shape. As always, my wife, Peg, has been a major help in diverse ways, particularly with the typing, proofreading, and indexing.

In conclusion, as someone once said—was it Aristotle, or Lawrence E. Thayer, or Grantland Rice, or perhaps De Wolf Hopper—if those who read this book enjoy it as much as I did writing it, they will enjoy it an awful lot.

PART ONE

THE HISTORICAL RECORD

Ernest Lawrence Thayer's 1888 ballad of baseball, "Casey at the Bat," has long occupied a place of prominence in the annals of American literature, sacred or profane. Whether it is epic verse or forgettable doggerel is not the major concern of this book. Its durability alone is sufficient to justify such a historical and literary query as is attempted here. Part one, "The Historical Record," considers the several controversies which the original poem generated. Part two, "The Literary Record," on the other hand, surveys the many poems that "Casey at the Bat" inspired and groups them into convenient categories.

De Wolf Hopper, a famous comic actor at the turn of the century, unquestionably rescued the verse from oblivion and gave it national recognition, but for a number of years a heated dispute centered over the authorship of the poem. Having no idea that he had penned a "classic," Thayer did not sign his name when it was first published. Using his usual pseudonym "Phin," he made no initial effort to identify himself with it. These circumstances allowed the authorship controversy to rage for many years.

Two additional disputes developed over specific elements in the poem. First, a number of old-time ballplayers named "Casey" claimed to be the prototype for Thayer's hero. Second, and less urgent, was the argument over the location of Mudville, the site of the famous strikeout. In this section, the circumstances attending the "debut" of "Casey" precede a discussion of the three controversies over authorship, "Casey," and Mudville.

1.

The Debut

On Sunday morning, June 3, 1888, the *San Francisco Examiner* published the following poem on page 4.

CASEY AT THE BAT

A Ballad of the Republic, Sung in the Year 1888

The outlook wasn't brilliant for the Mudville nine that day,
The score stood four to two with but one inning more to play;
And then when Cooney died at first and Barrows did the same,
A sickly silence fell upon the patrons of the game.

A straggling few got up to go in deep despair. The rest
Clung to that hope which springs eternal in the human breast;
They thought if only Casey could but get a whack at that—
We'd put up even money now with Casey at the bat.

But Flynn preceded Casey, as did also Jimmy Blake,
And the former was a lulu and the latter was a cake;
So upon that stricken multitude grim melancholy sat,
For there seemed but little chance of Casey's getting to the bat.

But Flynn let drive a single, to the wonderment of all,
And Blake, the much despised, tore the cover off the ball;
And when the dust had lifted, and the men saw what had occurred,
There was Jimmy safe at second and Flynn a-hugging third.

Then from 5,000 throats and more there rose a lusty yell,
It rumbled through the valley, it rattled in the dell;
It knocked upon the mountain and recoiled upon the flat,
For Casey, mighty Casey, was advancing to the bat.

There was ease in Casey's manner as he stepped into his place,
There was pride in Casey's bearing and a smile on Casey's face;
And when responding to the cheers, he lightly doffed his hat,
No stranger in the crowd could doubt 'twas Casey at the bat.

Ten thousand eyes were on him as he rubbed his hands with dirt,
Five thousand tongues applauded when he wiped them on his shirt;
Then while the writhing pitcher ground the ball into his hip,
Defiance gleamed in Casey's eye, a sneer curled Casey's lip.

And now the leather-covered sphere came hurtling through the air;
And Casey stood a-watching it in haughty grandeur there;
Close by the sturdy batsman the ball unheeded sped—
"That ain't my style," said Casey. "Strike one," the umpire said.

From the benches, black with people, there went up a muffled roar,
Like the beating of the storm-waves on a stern and distant shore;
"Kill him! Kill the umpire!" shouted some one on the stand,
And it's likely they'd have killed him had not Casey raised his hand.

With a smile of Christian charity great Casey's visage shone,
He stilled the rising tumult; he bade the game go on;
He signaled to the pitcher, and once more the spheroid flew,
But Casey still ignored it, and the umpire said, "Strike two."

"Fraud!" cried the maddened thousands, and echo answered fraud,
But one scornful look from Casey and the audience was awed;
They saw his face grow stern and cold, they saw his muscles strain,
And they knew that Casey wouldn't let that ball go by again.

The sneer is gone from Casey's lip, his teeth are clenched in hate,
He pounds with cruel violence his bat upon the plate;
And now the pitcher holds the ball, and now he lets it go,
And now the air is shattered by the force of Casey's blow.

Oh, somewhere in this favored land the sun is shining bright,
The band is playing somewhere, and somewhere hearts are light;
And somewhere men are laughing, and somewhere children shout,
But there is no joy in Mudville—mighty Casey has struck out.

—"Phin" [1]

"Phin" had written a number of other ballads during the previous six months for the *Examiner*.[2] It is not likely, however, that any of his ballads would be remembered today (and perhaps they are not) were it not for a fortuitous set of circumstances which occurred the following year.

Early in May 1889,[3] not quite a year after the publication of "Casey at the Bat," the McCaull Light Opera Company, owned by a Colonel McCaull, was about to open a new show at Wallack's Theater in New York City. Two of McCaull's young actors, Digby Bell and De Wolf Hopper, were great baseball fans. They were at the Polo Grounds almost every afternoon and for two years had put on annual benefit shows for the New York Giants.

By coincidence, "Cap" Anson's famous Chicago White Stockings and the Giants were meeting for a series of games the very week the show, *Prince Methusalem*, was to open. Bell and Hopper got the idea of a baseball night at Wallack's at which both the White Stockings and Giants, seated in long rows on opposite sides of the theater, would be honored guests. They proposed the plan to McCaull, who liked it. Thoughts that the presence of such heroes as Buck Ewing, Tim Keefe, and Anson would guarantee a full house no doubt danced through his mind. They picked the next Friday as "baseball night" and announced it in the local papers.

Archibald Clevering Gunter, a writer of some distinction in the 1880s and a devotee of baseball as well, read the notice and went to see McCaull.

"I've got just the thing for your baseball night," he said. "It's a baseball poem I cut out of a 'Frisco paper when I was on the coast last winter. I've been carrying it around ever since. It's a lulu, and young Hopper could do it a turn."

Gunter handed McCaull a wrinkled newspaper clipping, the original "Casey" poem which he had clipped from the *Examiner*. McCaull read it, jumped in glee, and agreed that Hopper should recite it on the baseball night. That same evening McCaull gave Hopper the poem and told him to have it ready for the big event. Hopper stuck it in his pocket and forgot about it, for the time being, that is. The Giants and White Stockings opened their series on Thursday, and of course Hopper was at the Polo Grounds. That night he received a telegram from his home in New England. His twenty-month-old son had contracted diphtheria, and the crisis would come before morning.

"I was frantic," he recalled. "I slept little that night and early Friday morning found me camping on the steps of Wallack's, directly across from the Western Union office. . . . There had been a violent storm in lower New England during the night, the wires were down in the morning and no word came."

When McCaull arrived around nine-thirty, Hopper was still sitting on Wallack's steps. He explained what had happened and declared, "I can't commit this piece. I can't call my name until I hear how the boy is."

"Surely, surely," replied McCaull. "Forget all about it, my boy."

Toward eleven o'clock, two telegraph operators came rushing across the street shouting Hopper's name. The crisis was passed, and the infant had survived. Hopper hurried into McCaull's office with the good news. After quieting down, he remembered the clipping.

"I'll study it now. Just give me the office to myself for awhile." McCaull cleared out and in less than an hour Hopper had memorized "Casey at the Bat."[4]

That night, during act 2 of *Prince Methusalem*, Hopper stopped the show with his first public rendition of "Casey." He remembered the occasion well.

On his debut Casey lifted this audience, composed largely of baseball players and fans, out of their seats. When I dropped my voice to B flat, below low C, and "the multitude was awed," I remember Buck Ewing's gallant mustachios give a single nervous twitch. And as the house, after a moment of startled silence, grasped the anti-climactic denouement, it shouted its glee. They had expected as anyone does on hearing Casey for the first time, that the mighty batsman would slam the ball out of the lot and a lesser bard would have had him do so, and thereby written merely a good sporting page filler.[5]

Although Thayer's poem had little effect on his own career, it transformed Hopper's life. "I thought at the time," he reminisced,

that I was merely repeating a poem, a fatherless waif clipped from a San Francisco newspaper. As it turned out I was launching a career, a career of declaiming those verses up and down this favored land the balance of my life. When my name is called upon the resurrection morn I shall very probably, unless some friend is there to pull the sleeve of my ascension robe, arise, clear my throat and begin: "The outlook wasn't brilliant for the Mudville nine that day."[6]

Although Hopper recognized at once that he had a "hot" item in "Casey," he had no thought of incorporating the poem into his regular routine for several years. One night during the 1892–1893 season, however, he decided the show needed a little brightening, so he trotted out "Casey." It was a big success, so he injected it into the program each night at some unexpected point. Often a show was not allowed to start until Hopper had satisfied the demands from the audience for "Casey." Wherever he went, whatever the show, "Casey" was the big moment of the evening for everyone. For the rest of his life, for over forty years, Hopper continued to recite the verse. He estimates that he delivered at least ten thousand renditions of "Casey," varying it frequently to keep himself from falling asleep. The time required for the thirteen stanzas was five minutes and forty seconds.[7]

Through all this one has to marvel at the role pure chance played in the publicizing of "Casey at the Bat." Had Archibald C. Gunter not been in San Francisco in June 1888 and seen the poem in the *Examiner*, he would not have been able to pass it on to Hopper in New York in 1889. And had Hopper and Bell not persuaded McCaull to hold a "baseball night" at Wallack's Theater, there would have been no occasion for reciting the verse. And had Hopper's son not passed the crisis of his illness when he did, Hopper would have had no reason to commit the verse to memory. Happily, all these things happened, and "Casey at the Bat" was saved for posterity.

But the ballad became mutilated at an early time, and a number of inaccurate versions soon got out and were accepted as the real thing. The most widely quoted corruption was published in Frederic Lawrence Knowles's *Treasury of*

Humorous Poetry. Among the various changes were a revised first line, an incorrect score, and a misspelled name for the first baseman. In fact, ''Burrows'' has appeared far more often than ''Barrows'' in the ''Casey'' literature. There are several other differences, particularly in the first five stanzas. Following is an early, corrupted version.

It looked extremely rocky for the Mudville nine that day,
The score stood four to six with but an inning left to play;
And so, when Cooney died at first, and Burrows did the same,
A pallor wreathed the features of the patrons of the game.

A straggling few got up to go, leaving there the rest,
With that hope which springs eternal within the human breast;
For they thought if only Casey could get a whack at that,
They'd put up even money with Casey at the bat.

But Flynn preceded Casey, and likewise so did Blake,
And the former was a pudding and the latter was a fake;
So on that stricken multitude a death-like silence sat,
For there seemed but little chance of Casey's getting to the bat.

But Flynn let drive a single to the wonderment of all,
And the much despised Blakey tore the cover off the ball;
And when the dust had lifted and they saw what had occurred,
There was Blakey safe on second, and Flynn a-hugging third.

Then from the gladdened multitude went up a joyous yell,
It bounded from the mountain top and rattled in the dell;
It struck upon the hillside, and rebounded on the flat,
For Casey, mighty Casey, was advancing to the bat.

There was ease in Casey's manner as he stepped into his place,
There was pride in Casey's bearing and a smile on Casey's face;
And when responding to the cheers he lightly doffed his hat,
No stranger in the crowd could doubt, 'twas Casey at the bat.

Ten thousand eyes were on him as he rubbed his hands with dirt,
Five thousand tongues applauded as he wiped them on his shirt;
And while the writhing pitcher ground the ball into his hip—
Defiance gleamed from Casey's eye—a sneer curled Casey's lip.

And now the leather-covered sphere came hurtling through the air,
And Casey stood a-watching it in haughty grandeur there;
Close by the sturdy batsman the ball unheeded sped—
''That hain't my style,'' said Casey—''Strike one,'' the umpire said.

From the bleachers black with people there rose a sullen roar,
Like the beating of the storm waves on a stern and distant shore;
"Kill him! kill the Umpire!" shouted some one from the stand—
And it's likely they'd have done it had not Casey raised his hand.

With a smile of Christian charity great Casey's visage shone,
He stilled the rising tumult and he bade the game go on;
He signalled to the pitcher and again the spheroid flew,
But Casey still ignored it and the Umpire said "Strike two."

"Fraud!" yelled the maddened thousands, and the echo answered "Fraud,"
But one scornful look from Casey and the audience was awed;
They saw his face grow stern and cold, they saw his muscles strain,
And they knew that Casey would not let that ball go by again.

The sneer is gone from Casey's lip, his teeth are clenched with hate,
He pounds with cruel violence his bat upon the plate;
And now the pitcher holds the ball, and now he lets it go,
And now the air is shattered by the force of Casey's blow.

Oh! somewhere in this favored land the sun is shining bright,
The band is playing somewhere, and somewhere hearts are light;
And somewhere men are laughing, and somewhere children shout,
But there is no joy in Mudville—mighty Casey has "Struck Out."[8]

2.

Search for the Author

While De Wolf Hopper founded a career on "Casey," he had no idea who had written the poem. It was not that he did not want to find out; he tried "desperately," in some accounts, to find the author. There appeared to be no way of tracing the clipping back to its original source since everyone had forgotten that it had first appeared in the *San Francisco Examiner*. Then one night while Hopper's troupe was performing the then popular comic opera *Wang* in Worcester, Massachusetts—it was in either 1892 or 1893—Hopper received a note from an old family acquaintance named Hammond. "Hammond wrote me," Hopper noted in his memoirs, "asking me to come to the Worcester Club after the performance. If I would do so he would introduce me to the author of Casey." [1]

It was a pleasant meeting, Hopper happy to know Ernest Thayer, the man who had supplied his trademark, and Thayer pleased to meet the chap who had publicized his verse. That evening several of the club members urged Thayer to recite portions of his comic writings, which he did with fair effectiveness. They insisted that Thayer do "Casey," but he declined, saying that "Casey" was Hopper's stunt. They continued their urgings and finally he gave in. Hopper writes: "I have heard many another give Casey. Fond mamas have brought their young sons to me to hear their childish voices lisp the poem, but Thayer's was the worst of all. In a sweet, dulcet, Harvard whisper he implored Casey to murder the umpire, and gave this cry of mass animal rage all the emphasis of a caterpillar wearing rubbers crawling on a velvet carpet. He was rotten!" [2] Thayer was much too shy and soft-spoken to satisfy the big, loud, outgoing Hopper.

Neither Hopper nor Thayer thought about the issue of authorship at that time or for some years to come. Having quit journalism to help supervise the family textile factory in Worcester, Thayer almost forgot he had written "Casey." Hopper continued to recite the poem at a developing pace of popularity, and by 1900 "Casey at the Bat" had become a national institution. In 1902, for the first time, the poem was included in a bound volume of verse—*A Treasury of Humorous Poetry*, edited by Frederic Lawrence Knowles. But alas, the author was identified as Joseph Quinlan Murphy. [3]

Over two years passed, and then Lee Goldberg, sportswriter for the *Louis-ville Herald*, wrote a lengthy discussion of "Casey's" authorship which *The Sporting News* reprinted early in 1905. Goldberg first recited Hopper's testimony that Thayer had written "Casey," but quickly added that Thayer was only one of several claimants. The most credible one, in Goldberg's opinion, was Will Valentine, lately deceased. Valentine had arrived in the United States from Ireland in 1876 and by the early 1880s was city editor of the *Kansas City Star*. In 1882 he assumed a similar post with the *Sioux City Tribune* in Iowa and began writing poems and parodies, all signed "February 14." Valentine roomed with Frank T. Wilstach, and one Sunday afternoon, while Wilstach was reading Thomas Babington Macaulay's "Horatius at the Bridge," he suggested to Valentine that "Horatius" would serve as an ideal model for a poem about a "Mick at the Bat." Valentine was taken by the idea and at once, according to Wilstach, composed "Casey at the Bat," which he stated appeared in the *Sioux City Tribune* the same year, 1882.[4]

Following Wilstach's lead, Goldberg expressed his conviction that "Casey" indeed was a parody of "Horatius." The fact that the words "the nine gods" appeared in the first line of "Horatius" suggested that this might have been the source for "the Mudville nine" in the first line of "Casey." Other parallels presented themselves, although "Horatius" was a much longer poem. For "Defiance gleamed in Casey's eye, a sneer curled Casey's lip," there was "He smiled on these bold Romans, a smile serene and high." For " 'Kill him! Kill the umpire!' someone shouted from the stand," there was " 'Down with Him!' cried false Sextus, with a smile on his pale face." Finally, for "And some-where men are laughing and somewhere children shout, There is no joy in Mudville—mighty Casey has struck out," there was "With weeping and with laughter, still is the story told, How well Horatius kept the bridge, in the brave days of old." "It is to be hoped in the future," concluded Goldberg, "that 'Casey at the Bat' may be credited to its rightful owner, the brilliant child of Erin, Will Valentine."[5]

Goldberg's flat assertion excited the sensibilities of Joseph M. Cummings, baseball writer for the *Baltimore News*. About the time that *The Sporting News* reprinted Goldberg's essay, Cummings met one Eben Sutton, a Thayer class-mate of 1885 at Harvard, who stated positively that Thayer had written "Casey." Sutton described Thayer's literary attainments as a Harvard undergraduate, in-cluding editorship of the *Lampoon* and Class Day Orator. Following gradua-tion, Sutton said, Thayer assumed a post as "Funny Man" on the *San Fran-cisco Examiner*, published by another of their classmates, William Randolph Hearst. While writing for the *Examiner* Thayer had composed "Casey at the Bat." To verify this story Cummings wrote to Thayer at his Worcester home, requesting supporting evidence that he had indeed been "Casey's" author. Cummings received the following letter:

Rome, Grand Hotel, Feb. 2, 1905. To the Sporting Editor of the News: Your letter of January 14, inquiring about the authorship of "Casey at the Bat" has just reached me.

I have seen the story of which you speak and which attributes the poem to a mythical Will Valentine. The statement that it was printed by him in the *Sioux City Tribune* in 1882 is absolutely false, as an examination of the files of that paper will certainly show. "Casey at the Bat" was first published in the *San Francisco Examiner* in 1888.

I cannot give the exact date, of course, but it was sometime in the spring or summer of that year. It was the last of many ballads—some better, some worse—that the *Examiner* printed from my pen during my connection with the paper in the capacity of "funny man," so called. These ballads were usually signed "Phin." . . . You ask me what incentive I had for writing "Casey." It was the same incentive that I had for writing a thousand other things. It was my business to write, and I needed the money.

There have been many claimants to the doubtful honor of having written "Casey at the Bat"—among others, I believe, the late Mike Kelly of Boston, and it has never seemed to me that it was worth my while to expose their impudence. But Will Valentine or his next friend is such a particularly atrocious liar—adducing as he does so many imaginary facts and placarding me by name as a cheap imposter—that I am reluctantly compelled to say something. I am obliged to you for writing to me, and hope you will give publicity to any part of this letter or to all of it, as you may think fit.[6]

Very shortly a second letter from Thayer in Rome, dated February 4, 1905, was received by Cummings, which he included in his article published by *The Sporting News*. It read:

Since writing you the other day other facts about "Casey" have occurred to me which perhaps will be of interest to you. Except as originally published in the *Examiner*, "Casey" has never been correctly printed—barring one or two cases in which I have furnished a copy. The reason for this I will explain. When the poem was first copied into an Eastern paper—I think by the *New York Sun*—the clipping editor cut off the opening stanzas and began where "Casey" advances to the bat. Later on De Wolf Hopper began to recite the complete poem as it was given to him by Mr. Archibald Gunter, who saw it in the *Examiner*. Someone who heard Hopper's rendition wrote out the first five stanzas from memory—and a very bad memory he must have had—tacked them to the mutilated version as it was printed in the *Sun* and many of its exchanges and then published a combination which has been printed up and down the land as "Casey at the Bat." I think that if the matter were of any importance the easiest way to establish the authorship would be to let the different claimants furnish a copy which might be compared with the poem as it was first printed in the *Examiner*. I may say, in conclusion, that, though some of the mutilated reprints of "Casey" have my name on the title page, I have never authorized them. I have left the poem to its fate—except that once I had a few copies printed for circulation among my friends, and only recently, when I am charged with falsely claiming the poem, has it seemed to me my duty to say something of my connection with it. Finally, while a certain Will Valentine may have written a baseball poem in a Sioux City paper before 1888, it could not have been "Casey at the Bat" and if anyone is anxious enough to search the files of that paper this fact will become patent."[7]

To check Thayer's claim, Cummings wrote to the *San Francisco Examiner* and asked that a search be made of the files for the "Casey" poem and that a copy of it be sent to him. Early in January 1906, E. B. Lenhart, assistant sporting editor of the paper, mailed the desired piece with the accompanying note: "Have carefully copied the original lines of Casey at the Bat from the *Examiner* on Sunday, June 3, 1888. The signature Phin was the pen name used by the late Phinney Thayer." Cummings now thought the evidence was complete. "The mystery of who wrote 'Casey at the Bat' has been solved."[8]

But it was not. And as Lee Allen wrote: "There must have been times in the life of Ernest Lawrence Thayer when he wished he had never written 'Casey at the Bat.' "[9] The swirling controversy prompted a writer in *Baseball Magazine*, a brand-new publication, to assert in 1908 that

A present day poet has not climbed very high on the ladder of fame unless honor of the authorship of the most famous bit of baseball verse has been flung on his shoulders. Everybody from Felicia Hemans to Boomerang Bolivar . . . has got in on it. . . . Literary critics from *The Atlantic Monthly* to the long-legged boy who gets the magazines for *The Podunk Appeal* have tried to unriddle the authorship of "Casey."[10]

By this time the principal contenders for the prize (besides Thayer) were Joseph Quinlan Murphy, Will Valentine, and a newcomer to the field, George Whitefield D'Vys of Cambridge, Massachusetts. Under challenge from these various quarters Thayer began pressing his claim more insistently. When Murphy was said to have been the author, he checked and found that Murphy had died. When he learned of Valentine's contention, he investigated and found that Valentine was also dead. Nevertheless he hired the law firm of his former classmate, Eugene Lent, in San Francisco, to pursue the matter directly in Sioux City. The search found nothing to support Valentine. And now D'Vys insisted that he had written the poem two years before it had appeared in the *Examiner*.

The question of "Casey's" authorship became so intense that there was a rising demand to ferret out the truth and put all doubts at rest. John W. Glenister, writing in *Baseball Magazine* in June 1908, reviewed the arguments of the various claimants. Although he leaned toward Thayer, he urged that the matter be settled once and for all. "Who did write 'Casey?' I don't know, but I do know that it is high time to settle this controversy that has been going on for years. I suggest that the claimants hand in their claims under sworn affidavits with all evidence to the editor of the *Baseball Magazine* at once. Then have a committee appointed to decide the case once and for all."[11]

The editor of *Baseball Magazine* did not act on the suggestion, but the editor of another monthly publication did. R. A. Davis, editor of *The Scrap Book*, greatly troubled by the ongoing controversy, launched an investigation. The results were published in the December 1908 issue. An explanatory note preceded the article.

For twenty years there has been carried on a sharp discussion as to who wrote the popular baseball lyric, "Casey at the Bat." The conclusions hitherto reached have been so unsatisfactory that the editor of *The Scrap Book* decided to have the controversy thoroughly sifted out and a definite result obtained. To this end the subject was turned over to Dr. Harry Thurston Peck, with the request that he follow up every possible clue and go to first-hand sources. As he is not acquainted with any of the claimants to the authorship of the poem, and as he has had long experience in literary investigation, it was felt that he would succeed in solving this much-vexed question with authority, and thereby lay it forever at rest. What follows is his report, made after the most painstaking and accurate research.[12]

Although Harry Peck, professor of Latin at Columbia University and popular historian at the turn of the century, quoted one of the corrupted versions of the poem and made several errors in describing the events surrounding the writing of "Casey," his findings were the most authoritative yet published on the subject. He first requested testimonial letters from three former Harvard classmates of Thayer who also worked with him on the *Examiner* at the time he wrote his ballads. The first of these, Eugene Lent, replied as follows:

. . . I can only say that the poem was written by Mr. Ernest Lawrence Thayer of Worcester, Massachusetts. I am under the impression that Mr. Thayer wrote "Casey at the Bat" at Worcester, and forwarded it by mail to the *Examiner . . .* because I was at Worcester with Thayer about the time he received a remittance from the *Examiner*, which was in payment of the poem.

Mr. Thayer is a graduate of Harvard of the class of '85, and during the last three years at Cambridge he was president of the Harvard *Lampoon*. A reference to the files of the *Lampoon* for the years '83, '84, and '85 will give one an idea of Thayer's versatility in literature.

After graduation, Thayer spent a year or more in Paris, and from that city contributed a series of letters to the *San Francisco Examiner*. He then came to San Francisco and did routine journalistic work on the *Examiner*, as well as being part of its editorial staff, for a year or more.

The Sunday Supplement in those days, for the greater part, was written by the regular employees of the paper, and Thayer had a regular column to fill every Sunday, which he did under the name of "Phin."

Thayer also contributed a series of ballads every other Sunday for quite a period of time, and many humorous poems, none of which, however, ever attained the popularity of "Casey at the Bat."[13]

Another old friend, journalist Lewis J. Stellmann, wrote that "there is no reasonable doubt in the minds of old-time newspaper men here [in San Francisco] that E. L. Thayer is the only and original author of 'Casey at the Bat.' "[14] A third testimonial came from Theodore F. Bonnet, who remembered that he "was doing baseball for the *Examiner* when young Hearst came out from Harvard to manage the paper. He brought with him E. L. Thayer, better known as 'Phinney' Thayer. . . . There can be no doubt of his authorship, and it is only because Thayer is such a modest, easy-going chap that a prompt and emphatic denial did not dispose of the question, once and for all, years ago."[15] From these letters Peck reached the tentative conclusion that "Casey at the Bat" first appeared in the *San Francisco Examiner*, June 3, 1888, and that the author was Thayer.[16]

Peck next analyzed the claims of the other contenders for authorship honors. Joseph Quinlan Murphy's claim was found in the aforementioned Knowles anthology. Knowles and Murphy were now dead and for all the help the publishers of the book—Dana, Estes and Company of Boston—gave Peck, they might as well have been dead too. They professed ignorance on the subject believing only that Knowles "always was particular to trace anything of which he made use as accurately as possible."[17] Since no evidence was supplied to support Murphy's case, Peck felt compelled to reject it. The claims of the next writer, William Valentine, have already been stated. Valentine supposedly published the poem in the *Sioux City Tribune* either in 1882 or 1886, prior to Thayer's work in the *Examiner*. Peck had the files of that paper checked and the Valentine-Wilstach poem was not found.[18]

This left George W. D'Vys, the most persistent and newest claimant. Peck wrote to D'Vys, in Cambridge, Massachusetts, and asked him to explain his case. He replied in verbose detail. After describing his early years, his knack for "versifying," and his love of baseball, he spoke of a Sunday ride out to Franklin Park in suburban Boston.

I tossed myself upon a knoll overlooking a ball field. While reclining there and musing, I suddenly observed the diamond. It was all evolution. From there I was wafted to the dear old South End ballgrounds—Boston—and there flashed to memory a day I should never forget, when at a crisis a noted player *fanned* and dashed all hope. Then came thoughts of the "King," Mike Kelly, and quickly I was *all* baseball, and then like a flash the incident I have referred to went into a rime. I was fairly wild as it mapped out itself—yes, wild. I wasn't a newspaper correspondent in those days so had neither notebook nor pencil to jot down what was in my head; but I said it over and over again to "keep it."

Ed [his friend, Edward L. Cleveland] came back and had a pencil, but no paper. Over the field came flying a portion of someone's Sunday *Globe*. I secured it, and then in the margin wrote the first and last words of each line and put the memoranda in my pocket. Ed was as wild over that rime as myself, and when I got home I wrote it—"There was ease in Casey's manner," etc., and the 32-lines I sent to Mr. O. P. Caylor of the New York *Sporting Times*, of which I held his red card credentials as correspondent.

Yes, sir, I wrote "Casey" as then printed. Who tacked on the front end, I cannot say.[19]

In analyzing this statement Peck noted that D'Vys only claimed title to the last eight stanzas, not the entire verse. Peck wrote to Edward L. Cleveland at Shelby, Montana, for verification of D'Vys's story. Cleveland responded, after a delay, explaining that he wanted to check the copy of "Casey" which Peck had against "what I *know* to be the original, written by George W. D'Vys one Sunday p.m. the last of September 1889, in Franklin Park. . . . I remember it very distinctly, for the circumstances connected therewith made me, in a way, instrumental in leading him to write it."[20]

Peck observed that although Cleveland agreed that D'Vys wrote the poem, he stated that it was composed in September 1889, three years after D'Vys's date, and over a year after the poem appeared in the *Examiner*. Peck further explored D'Vys's statement that he sent his eight stanzas to O. P. Caylor of the *Sporting Times* of New York. He learned that Caylor was dead, that the *Sporting Times* had ceased publication many years before, and that it would be very difficult to try and track down any copies for August 1886. A Boston lawyer told Peck that he had "hunted high and low" for copies, even advertising in the papers, but all in vain.[21]

Having carefully weighed all of his evidence, Peck decided that before he reached a final judgment, he should put the matter in judicial form and request notarized statements from both Thayer and D'Vys. Thayer replied immediately, in a statement notarized by one Charles F. Aldrich.

All of the thirteen stanzas composing the ballad . . . were written by me for the *San Francisco Examiner* in the spring of 1888, and were published, I think, on the third of June in that year. . . . I went to San Francisco in the summer of 1886 at the request of W. R. Hearst for the purpose of joining the staff of the *Examiner*. . . . Young Hearst had associated with me at Harvard College in the publication of the *Lampoon*, and when, immediately after leaving college, the *Examiner* fell into his hands, he asked me and two other college friends . . . to come out and lend him a hand. I was in San Francisco until the winter of 1887–1888, when my health gave out and I was obliged to return East. When connected with the *Examiner* I wrote a great deal for all departments of the paper, but my most successful contributions were a series of ballads which were begun in the fall of 1887, and continued on Sundays for the rest of the year. After I returned home I still occasionally sent something to the *Examiner*, and "Casey at the Bat" was, I think, the last thing which I sent. . . .

Notary Aldrich appended his own testimonial that Thayer was a man of impeccable honor and that he had known for at least fifteen years that Thayer had written "Casey at the Bat."[22]

In contrast to Thayer's prompt and forthright affidavit, D'Vys equivocated. First, he sent a letter saying that he was ill but that he would submit a sworn statement as soon as possible. Within a couple of weeks, he wrote that he had gone to Boston to search out a certain justice of the peace familiar with his family, but could not locate him. Two weeks later D'Vys sent Peck an unsworn document almost identical with his first letter. In the first line of this statement he had originally written "I . . . do hereby swear. . . . " Before mailing it, however, he erased "swear" and substituted "declare." The erasure marks were easily visible to Peck.[23]

D'Vys began by repeating the story contained in his first letter about writing the poem in 1886 at Franklin Park and submitting it to the *Sporting Times*, which published it shortly thereafter. He then wrote of a later time, the spring of 1897, when the piece appeared in the *Boston Globe* with five additional stanzas tacked on in front and the whole work attributed to someone else. This irked him, so the next day he sent his mother to the *Globe* office—he himself was disabled by a recent injury—taking with her his only copy of the *Sporting Times* containing the poem and two letters from O. P. Caylor authenticating his authorship. D'Vys's mother was assured that her "boy" would get justice, but when she left the *Globe* office she unfortunately forgot to take the "proof positive" with her. The father was ill at the time, so the "Casey" matter was temporarily forgotten. When D'Vys himself felt better he went to the *Globe* office to secure the proofs, but got no help in locating his materials.[24]

D'Vys next told of an earlier Sunday afternoon, in May 1885, when he and his mother were resting on Cambridge Common. She was reading the *Globe*, while he scribbled "love ditties and baseball rimes" in a little book. One of the love verses referred to a dear friend who was leaving for a vacation.

O, somewhere in this mighty land, the sun is shining bright,
And somewhere hearts are happy, and somewhere hearts are light;
The band is playing somewhere and children romp and play,
But there's no joy for poor G. D. since N. A. went away!

He remembered that poem at a later time when he wrote "Casey." His baseball poems were based on his play experiences as a boy in an area of the city of Somerville known as "Mudville." And on that Sunday afternoon in 1885 his thoughts ran to his hero, Mike "King" Kelly, and he wrote a baseball verse based on an incident he had recently witnessed:

There was ease in Kelly's manner, when he stepped into his place,
There was pride in Kelly's bearing and a smile on Kelly's face;
And when, responding to the cheers, he lightly doffed his hat,
No stranger in the crowd could doubt 'twas Kelly at the bat!

D'Vys said he continued writing the poem—"I just *couldn't stop* until came the climax"—and when he was done he knew it was good. He signed it "anon" because his "stern" father did not want him to write poetry.[25]

Just as he finished composing the verse, a runaway horse dashed by, and D'Vys and his mother, forgetting everything else, went chasing after the runaway. When they finally returned to their place on Cambridge Common, to their consternation they found not only that mother's *Globe* was gone, but also the little book of rhymes. Unfortunately, D'Vys had neglected to put his name in the book so it would be almost impossible to identify and reclaim it. He was convinced that the imposter who claimed to have written "Casey at the Bat" was the same person who had absconded with his rhyme book.[26]

Since this document was not an affidavit and without legal standing in any court, Peck again wrote D'Vys requesting a sworn statement. Following further delays and "explanatory" letters, D'Vys finally sent Peck this notarized form:

Personally appeared before me, a Notary Public, for and within the Commonwealth of Massachusetts, George D'Vys of Cambridge, Massachusetts, and made oath that the statement recently made by him to Professor Harry Thurston Peck, New York City, to be published in *The Scrap Book*, in relation to that portion of the baseball ballad known as "Casey at the Bat" is a true statement of the facts.

Signed Thomas W. Spencer.[27]

Having digested all of this information, Peck set forth six facts as "definitely established."

(1) The full thirteen stanzas of "Casey at the Bat" appeared in the *San Francisco Examiner* of June 3, 1888, and were contributed to that paper by Mr. Ernest L. Thayer, of Worcester, Massachusetts, at that time a contributor to the *Examiner*, over the pseudonym of "Phin." (2) The poem cannot be shown to have appeared in any authentic publication before that date; while afterward it was not only published in many newspapers, but was recited by Mr. De Wolf Hopper on the stage. (3) No claimant for the authorship can produce a copy of the poem in the files of any magazine or newspaper prior to its appearance in the *Examiner*. (4) Mr. George W. D'Vys asserts that he wrote eight stanzas of it in August, 1886, and summons Mr. Edward L. Cleveland as a witness to the fact. Mr. Cleveland, however, gives a different date, and says that he positively knows Mr. D'Vys to have first shown him the poem in September, 1889, more than three years later. (5) Mr. Thayer makes a definite affidavit to the truth of his story before a notary public. Mr. D'Vys, after a long delay, sends an unsworn declaration, and that after a second delay sends an attestation in which his declaration is not incorporated; nor is the form of attestation a usual one, in that it is not signed by Mr. D'Vys. (6) With regard to the internal evidence, it seems obvious to me that the author of the first five stanzas must be the same person as the one who wrote the last eight stanzas. The whole poem, in fact, constitutes what a modern critic of French literature has aptly styled "a seamless unity." Furthermore, the writings of Mr. Thayer, both in the Harvard *Lampoon* and the *San Francisco Examiner*, show humor, facility of expression, and literary skill, such as one might expect from the author of "Casey at the Bat." On the other hand, whatever Mr. D'Vys has written and published falls below this literary standard, and affords no evidence that he could have written so popular and spirited a ballad.[28]

One other detailed study of the authorship issue was made by writer and critic Burton Egbert Stevenson in 1923. Stevenson came to his task in the course of researching materials for an intriguing little volume he called *Famous Single Poems*. The point of the book was that these were the only poems of significance the authors ever wrote; that is, "Casey" was Thayer's "only" poem. Stevenson reviewed the circumstances attending the writing of each of the fifteen poems in his book and in the course of his investigation came across the "Casey" controversy. He made his own study of the matter, and the results, later incorporated in his book, were first published in the *New York Herald*, January 14, 1923.[29]

Proceeding chronologically, the first claimant, again, was Joseph Quinlan Murphy of St. Louis. Like Peck before him, Stevenson found out that Murphy and Frederic L. Knowles were both dead and that the publishers of Knowles's anthology, which attributed "Casey" to Murphy, were of no help. He looked into the "writers" section of Francis Richter's *History and Records of Baseball*, published in 1914, and found that a Joseph Murphy had at one time been on the staff of the *St. Louis Globe-Democrat*. This Murphy, however, did not have Quinlan for a middle name, spent a great deal of his time judging horse races, and never claimed to have written "Casey." Thus the Murphy claim had to remain, if not totally dismissed, at least unproven. The publishers of *A Treasury of Humorous Poetry*, Stevenson noted, "evidently concluded that Mr. Knowles had made a mistake, for in recent editions of the book, the poem is credited to Ernest L. Thayer." [30]

In examining the Valentine claim, Stevenson wrote to Wilstach, who replied in two letters. In letter one Wilstach changed the date of Valentine's arrival at the *Sioux City Tribune* from 1882 to 1885, but repeated essentially the same account as contained in Lee Goldberg's story in the *Louisville Herald*. Wilstach added that he ran into Valentine in New York City in 1898, by which time the latter was writing for the *New York World*. Valentine was peeved at Hopper's claim that Thayer had written "Casey" and asked Wilstach to confirm that he had suggested to him that he write a parody of "Horatius." Wilstach said he did remember that, but stopped short of saying that "Casey" was written by Valentine. In his second letter to Stevenson, however, he made that assertion.

This matter of "Casey at the Bat" is so nebulous that I would really like to withdraw from it. However, I am certain of two things: first, that I suggested to Will Valentine that he write a burlesque of Macaulay's "Horatius at the Bridge"; second, that he did write this burlesque and that it was called "Casey at the Bat." I was present in the room when he wrote it. I haven't seen his copy since that afternoon, or a day or two afterwards, when it appeared in the *Tribune*. Whether the present "Casey at the Bat" is a rewrite of Valentine's I can't say. [31]

Stevenson observed next that representatives of Eugene Lent had checked out the *Sioux City Tribune* and had not found Valentine's "Casey," but he was not content with that. He requested John H. Kelly, editor of the *Tribune*, to make an issue-by-issue search of their files to ascertain if indeed the paper had ever published "Casey at the Bat." Kelly replied as follows: "We have had one of our men go over every copy of the *Tribune* during 1885–1888 inclusive . . . but did not find the much sought 'Casey at the Bat.' It would have been a very real pleasure and distinction to have claimed the great 'Casey.' " [32]

Stevenson had little sympathy for D'Vys's labored explanations found in Harry Peck's *Scrap Book* article. Among other things, he found it hard to believe that D'Vys, aged twenty-six in 1886, feared that a "stern parent" might learn that he wrote poetry. "One might suppose," he commented, "he would have somewhat outgrown his awe of the stern parent." More incredible, however, was the unending string of misfortunes which beset D'Vys's documents attesting to his "Casey" authorship. When his mother visited the *Boston Globe* office in 1897 carrying with her a copy of the *Sporting Times* containing the poem and two letters from Caylor, she left without the "proof positive" and D'Vys was unable to get the materials back. And how "unfortunate" it was that his little book of "love ditties" had been pilfered from Cambridge Common. All of this moved Stevenson to observe that D'Vys "certainly had a run of bad luck!"[33]

With respect to the *Sporting Times*, Stevenson learned of a man who had a fairly good file of the paper. This gentleman advised him that the *Sporting Times* did not commence publication until March 6, 1887, many months after D'Vys claimed it had published his poem. Second, it came out that O. P. Caylor, with whom D'Vys said he had correspondence proving his authorship of "Casey," did not become the editor of the *Sporting Times* until 1890, four years after D'Vys's 1886 publication date. Moreover, it was shown that on July 29, 1888, the *Sporting Times* did publish the last eight stanzas of "Casey," although substituting the name of Kelly, but with an explanatory note saying the verse was "adapted from the *San Francisco Examiner.*"[34]

In addition to the mass of external evidence, the internal evidence provided further proof against D'Vys's claim. D'Vys argued that he wrote only the last eight stanzas; he did not know who wrote the first five. However, observed Stevenson, in agreement with Peck, "an examination of the poem will convince anyone that it was written by one man. It is an entity in style and manner. More than that, the poem is incomplete without the first five stanzas, which describe the situation at the moment Casey goes to bat and are necessary to an understanding of it."[35]

The controversy flared up briefly in 1932 when D'Vys, the "persistent and undiscouraged claimant," again argued in the pages of the *New York Times* that he was the author of "Casey at the Bat" and that it had been first published in the *Sporting Times* in 1886. This got Thayer's back up once more and he wrote a letter of denial from Santa Barbara, California, his retirement home. He pointed out that the *Sporting Times* was not in existence in 1886 and that it did publish a modified version of "Casey" in 1888, but attributed it to the *San Francisco Examiner*. He also reminded the readers that Harry Peck, in the 1908 *Scrap Book* article, had "reached the conclusion that for this, perhaps the greatest of my sins, I was exclusively to blame."[36]

The final chapter in the debate took place in the pages of *The Sporting News* in the spring of 1938. It was precipitated by the appearance of the old ballplayer Dan Casey on Gabriel Heatter's radio program, "We the People," on March 3. Casey told Heatter that he was the model for the protagonist in the famous poem. In its account of the broadcast *The Sporting News* commented, incidentally, that Thayer was the author of "Casey at the Bat." This elicited a strong protest from the unyielding D'Vys. He made the same old arguments he had made before, totally unintimidated by the weight of authority against his claim. The debate inspired articles in the paper by Fred Hoey, a New England sports announcer, and Fred Mosebach, a columnist for the *San Antonio Express*, both of whom supported Thayer. Neither Hoey nor Mosebach, however, added anything to the discussion, Hoey simply reciting Peck's argument, and Mosebach recalling a statement made many years before by Albert G. Spalding.[37]

Thayer and D'Vys would argue their cases no more. In a rather suprising sequence of events, both men died within about nine months of each other. Thayer was the first to go, at Santa Barbara, August 21, 1940, while D'Vys died at Northampton, Massachusetts, on May 30, 1941. Thayer was 77 and D'Vys 81.[38]

While Thayer was not happy with the several corruptions of his famous poem, he revised it once himself. This revision is not considered, for the most part, an improvement on the original, but it was his own favorite. When Stevenson was preparing to include "Casey at the Bat" in his *Famous Single Poems*, Thayer requested that the revised version, which first appeared in *The Bookman* in 1909, be used.[39]

> The outlook wasn't brilliant for the Mudville nine that day,
> The score stood four to two, with but one inning more to play;
> And then when Cooney died at first, and Barrows did the same,
> A pall-like silence fell upon the patrons of the game.
>
> A straggling few got up to go in deep despair. The rest
> Clung to that hope which springs eternal in the human breast;
> They thought, "If only Casey could but get a whack at that—
> We'd put up even money now, with Casey at the bat."
>
> But Flynn preceded Casey, as did also Jimmy Blake,
> And the former was a hoodoo, while the latter was a cake;
> So upon that stricken multitude grim melancholy sat,
> For there seemed but little chance of Casey getting to the bat.
>
> But Flynn let drive a single, to the wonderment of all,
> And Blake, the much despised, tore the cover off the ball;
> And when the dust had lifted, and men saw what had occurred,
> There was Jimmy safe at second and Flynn a-hugging third.
>
> Then from five thousand throats and more there rose a lusty yell,
> It rumbled through the valley, it rattled in the dell;
> It pounded on the mountain and recoiled upon the flat,
> For Casey, mighty Casey, was advancing to the bat.

There was ease in Casey's manner as he stepped into his place,
There was pride in Casey's bearing and a smile lit Casey's face;
And when, responding to the cheers, he lightly doffed his hat,
No stranger in the crowd could doubt 'twas Casey at the bat.

Ten thousand eyes were on him as he rubbed his hands with dirt,
Five thousand tongues applauded when he wiped them on his shirt;
Then while the writhing pitcher ground the ball into his hip,
Defiance flashed in Casey's eye, a sneer curled Casey's lip.

And now the leather-covered sphere came hurtling through the air,
And Casey stood a-watching it in haughty grandeur there;
Close by the sturdy batsman the ball unheeded sped—
"That ain't my style," said Casey. "Strike one!" the umpire said.

From the benches, black with people, there went up a muffled roar,
Like the beating of the storm-waves on a stern and distant shore;
"Kill him! Kill the umpire!" shouted some one on the stand,
And it's likely they'd have killed him had not Casey raised his hand.

With a smile of Christian charity great Casey's visage shone,
He stilled the rising tumult, he bade the game go on;
He signaled to the pitcher, and once more the dun sphere flew,
But Casey still ignored it, and the umpire said, "Strike two!"

"Fraud!" cried the maddened thousands, and echo answered, "Fraud!"
But one scornful look from Casey and the audience was awed;
They saw his face grow stern and cold, they saw his muscles strain,
And they knew that Casey wouldn't let that ball go by again.

The sneer has fled from Casey's lip, his teeth are clenched in hate,
He pounds with cruel violence his bat upon the plate;
And now the pitcher holds the ball, and now he lets it go,
And now the air is shattered by the force of Casey's blow.

Oh, somewhere in this favored land the sun is shining bright,
The band is playing somewhere, and somewhere hearts are light;
And somewhere men are laughing, and little children shout,
But there is no joy in Mudville—great Casey has struck out.[40]

3.
Who Was "Casey"?

Thayer's famous poem prompted a number of old ballplayers named "Casey," and one named something else, to claim that they were the original "Casey." For a time these claims were so widespread and insistent that one writer called the epidemic "worse than a plague of measles."[1] Four of the claimants advanced arguments serious enough to attract attention and win converts. They were John Patrick Parnell Cahill, Daniel Maurice Casey, O. Robinson Casey, and Dennis Patrick Casey.

First in the chronological list was Cahill. Listed in the *Baseball Encyclopedia* as John Francis Cahill, but also known as John Patrick Parnell Cahill, he was a fairly good player on the Pacific Coast in the 1880s. He also played three years in the major leagues with Columbus of the American Association in 1884, St. Louis of the National League in 1886, and Indianapolis of the National League in 1887. He was small, fast, a good base runner, and a pretty fair outfielder, but a weak hitter. His lifetime major league average for 252 games was only .205.[2]

Cahill played with Stockton in the California League prior to his major league experience, and since Stockton claimed to be the original Mudville, it was only fitting that Stockton claimed "Casey" in the person of Cahill as well. The big game, it was said, was played in Stockton in the spring of 1888 between an all-star aggregation of big leaguers and the Stockton team. Cahill supposedly played with the all-stars against his former club that day and struck out. Stockton won 4–2. Thayer supposedly saw the game and composed his epic. Further support for the Cahill-Stockton theory lay in the four names used by Thayer: Cooney, Barrows, Blake, and Flynn. Players with these names actually played in the California League at this time, although no two were on the same team. Thayer, it was intimated, picked those names at random from box scores of league games.[3]

Problems arose at once. First, the time of the game—the spring of 1888. Thayer returned East in February 1888 and probably composed the poem before this all-star game was played. Furthermore, if Cahill was not playing for the home team and the home team won, why was there such sorrow when he struck out? There should have been great jubilation. And why did not Thayer call his hero, Cahill, if indeed Cahill were "Casey?" The Stockton claim to being Mudville will be examined in the next chapter, but it is sufficient to say that it was linked closely with the Cahill claim. If one falls, the other goes down with it.

Cahill died in Pleasanton, California, on Friday, November 1, 1901. A week or so later *The Sporting News* reprinted a story about Cahill which first appeared in the *Chicago Record-Herald*. The story revealed more about the "Casey" mystery than about Cahill, but needs repeating here.

Casey is dead again—"Casey at the Bat"—the mighty Casey who set the world awry by striking out at Mudville. This time he is said to be totally dead, with no chance to appeal to the umpire of Destiny for a change of decision.

"Casey" has been dying at intervals ever since De Wolf Hopper made him famous by reciting that anonymous classic of the diamond. . . . But Casey would not remain extinct for any reasonable length of time, so people have come to doubt the sincerity of his dying "stunts." Heretofore he has always had something up his sleeve or a confederate behind the wings. The latest shuffling off was done at Pleasanton, California, which is bidding for some of the fame of Mudville. He didn't die under the name of "Casey" at all. On his coffin lid is inscribed the name "John Patrick Parnell Cahill." The cause of death, according to dispatches, was consumption. . . . The California man is really and completely dead. On that point all are agreed, but was he "Casey"?[4]

It is not known when Cahill first advanced his claim, or just how seriously he advanced it. In 1911 Albert G. Spalding published his big baseball history, *America's National Game*, and he included a few pages on the "Casey" question. He reprinted an undated newsclipping on the death of Cahill which was passed along to him by "Father" Chadwick. The story dealt with De Wolf Hopper, chiefly, but contained several lines pertinent to this discussion. "The Casey who just died was John Patrick Parnell Cahill, a former baseball player. On the Pacific Coast he was very popular as a player, and after his retirement from the diamond still held his head high, for he had been perpetuated in verse under the name of Casey."[5]

Spalding was convinced that Cahill was the model for Thayer's hero. He may have had more evidence than this lonely newsclipping for his conviction, but if he did he never shared it with anyone. In 1914 an old west coast fan and former player, Winfield Scott, met Spalding in San Diego, and the subject of "Casey" came up in the course of their conversation. Spalding reiterated to Scott what he had written in the book—that Cahill was "Casey" and that he died of tuberculosis in 1901. Scott wrote authoritatively in 1923 that Cahill was the original "Casey," that the issue was settled, and wondered why the question should be raised again.[6]

The second to the last paragraph of the *Chicago Record-Herald* story quoted above contained a significant passage.

And if it really be "Casey" whose soul went out with the tide in the sunny shores of the Pacific [referring to Cahill's death] what becomes of the claim of Daniel Casey, the streetcar conductor of Binghamton, New York? Here was a gentleman of Celtic name, who was scalped something like a year ago [1900] when his head came in contact with an overhanging trolley wire. He said he was the original and only Casey, but he didn't die, and thereby his claim was much discounted, but not before Hopper and Anson and a few other old friends sent touching messages of condolence and Daniel had been advertised from Maine to Mexico.[7]

Daniel Maurice Casey, one of three baseball brothers, was born in Binghamton October 2, 1865. He was a left-handed pitcher who compiled an average mark in seven years of big-league pitching. The record books are very inconsistent in their figures on Dan Casey, but according to the *Baseball Encyclopedia* he won ninety-six games and lost ninety. Most of his success was with the Philadelphia National League club in 1886, 1887, and 1888. His best year was 1887, when he won twenty-eight and lost thirteen. His last major league season was 1890, after which he played several more years in the minors with the Syracuse club. He was a weak hitter, with a lifetime average of .183.[8]

For many years it was believed that Dan Casey never advanced his claim until late in life that he was *the* "Casey." However, *The Sporting News*'s account of Cahill's death makes it clear that Dan Casey was one of the early claimants for the distinction. Apparently he was badly hurt in 1900 when struck by a trolley wire, and as he lay stricken he announced that he was the original "Casey." Little more was heard of Dan Casey's claim for some time.[9] Following his retirement from baseball in the 1890s, Casey got a job as a street railway conductor in Binghamton and played a fairly active role in the municipal affairs of that city. The Municipal League honored him on his forty-fifth birthday for his service to that organization. He was presented with a gold watch.[10] Casey retired from the street railroad in 1929 and moved to Washington, D.C.

Then in 1938 Dan Casey became a celebrity. One day early in that year he left his Silver Spring, Maryland, home—where "he trimmed his hedges and tended his roses"—and went into a Washington newspaper office. He told the writers there that he was the real "Casey" and then described the situation on which he insisted Thayer had based his epic. He convinced a few important people, including the well-known radio announcer Gabriel Heatter, that his story had merit. Heatter invited Casey to tell his story on "We the People," and on March 3, 1938, he did.

It was August 21, 1887. I was pitching for the Phillies. One hot summer afternoon we were playing the New York Giants in the old Philadelphia ball park. It was the last of the ninth and the score was 4 to 3 in favor of the Giants. Two men out, runners on second and third and my turn at bat. Folks, I was scared. The fans were cheering for me to knock it over the fence. It sure was an exaggeration to call me Mighty Casey. I never batted better than .183. But the week before, I busted up a game in Boston with a lucky homer and the fans wanted me to repeat. I looked at the pitcher [Tim Keefe] and he looked at me. I got a sort of sinking feeling.

Then the first ball came over. It was fast and looked a little low. I just stood lookin'. The poem says: "Close by the sturdy batsman the ball unheeded sped—That ain't my style, said Casey, 'Strike one,' the umpire said," and he was right. I never even got my bat off my shoulder. Then the New York catcher signalled for the next pitch. The poem says about that catcher: "He signalled to the pitcher, and once more the spheroid flew, but Casey still ignored it and the umpire cried 'Strike two.' " I hadn't ignored it. I just couldn't see it. Then I got plenty scared. Two men on bases—two strikes on me—and the last inning. I knew I had to swing at the next ball. The pitcher wound up and I saw that ball coming at me like a bullet. I swung that bat as hard as I could. I guess you know the rest.

I've been waiting 50 years to tell you folks that Mighty Casey was just old Dan Casey, a pretty good ballplayer, but no home run king. But I guess if I hadn't struck out that day I never would have become famous.[11]

Casey supported his claim by asserting that the area around the Philadelphia ball park at the time was called "Mudville." This was correct for, when Albert Reach and Colonel John I. Rogers purchased the land from the Philadelphia and Reading Railroad, it was indeed a vast, muddy morass. He further insisted that the Flynn and Blake who preceded him in the batting order were none other than the Phillies's seventh and eighth hitters, Charley Bastian and Joe Mulvey.[12]

The radio appearance of Dan Casey evoked a chorus of protest among the disbelievers. First, it was pointed out that the Phillies and Giants did not play on August 21, 1887, although they did meet the day before. Moreover, rather than being the villain of that game of August 20, Casey was the batting hero. He drove out a two-run single in the last of the ninth to tie the score 5–5. The game was called because of darkness at the end of ten innings—the score still tied.[13]

Among "Casey's" critics was Frank C. Payne, a former Chicago writer, who argued that Mike "King" Kelly, the great Chicago-Boston catcher, was the real model for "Casey," so no one named Casey could possibly be "Casey." Another baseball writer, Si Goodfriend, supported Payne's statement. Goodfriend said that he was present the night Hopper first delivered the poem at Wallack's Theater, and that Hopper changed the name from "Kelly"—that being the name in the poem—to "Casey" in order not to offend the "King" who was in the audience.[14]

With all of these challenges, Dan Casey's claim became somewhat tarnished. Nevertheless, he was awarded a silver lifetime pass to all major league games on the strength of his story. In addition, the International League Baltimore Orioles decided to stage a reenactment of the "mighty miss." One night during the 1938 season when the Jersey City Giants were in town, seventy-three-year-old Dan Casey stepped to the plate. An Oriole coach, Rogers Hornsby, toed the mound. Casey took the first pitch, a strike. Hornsby wound up and fired again. Casey swung and hit a weak roller to the shortstop. When queried by the press, he explained his failure to strike out: "Hornsby didn't have as much on the ball as Tim Keefe did."[15] Dan Casey died in Washington on February

8, 1943, still insisting on his claim. His obituary in *The Sporting News* covered nearly three columns.[16]

The third major claimant was a fellow named O. Robinson Casey, who played a few games with Detroit in 1882. Robinson advanced his claim in 1923. He lived in Syracuse, New York, and for years was president of the local chapter of the Society for the Prevention of Cruelty to Animals. He died in 1936 in Syracuse. Robinson contended that while with Detroit in the National League in 1885, he struck out with the bases loaded in a game against Minneapolis.[17]

Several flaws were spotted at once in this story which caused A. H. Tarvin to dismiss it as "merely another claim, that and nothing more." First, the only Casey on the Detroit team in 1885 was Dan Casey, who went over to Philadelphia the following year. Next, Minneapolis was not in the National League in 1885. Further, in *the* game the bases were not loaded.[18] In defense of this "Casey," however, it should be remembered that many persons involved in the "Casey" story got their dates mixed up. Also, Robinson did play with Detroit in 1882 and was with the Minneapolis club of the Northwestern League in 1884, the two teams mentioned in his story. The Northwestern League included half a dozen teams from Michigan in 1884 and perhaps he had one of those in mind. At any rate, while some event in Robinson's career might have been at least as close to Thayer's incident as Dan Casey's experience, both claims were considered pretty farfetched.[19]

The final of the four "Casey" claimants, Dan's older brother Dennis, never made the claim himself. His argument was advanced many years later by James Bready, a Baltimore writer, in a pictorial history of the Orioles. Dennis, an outfielder, played with Baltimore in the American Association in 1884 and 1885. Bready cited passages from news accounts of games to illustrate Dennis's hitting, fielding, and other skills. In one game he led the inning off with a home run, which unnerved the opposing pitcher and thus sparked a winning rally. On another occasion he won the game with a three-run, inside-the-park homer, whereby he demonstrated his great speed. He combined fielding and hitting and speed one day by making "two three-base hits and six fine fly catches." In a game with St. Louis, Casey robbed an opponent of a triple with "the finest one-hand running catch of the season." In that same game he also stroked two triples as the Orioles routed the Browns 15–0.[20]

Dennis joined the Orioles in mid-season of 1884 and provided a spark which boosted the club into the first division, the highest position it had ever achieved. Casey's valuable bat carried the team well into the 1885 season. But then problems developed. Here is how Bready described the situation.

In the summer of 1885, Casey had a run-in with Manager Bill Barnie. The Orioles had scheduled an exhibition game against a team of amateurs in Westminster, Maryland. Somehow, the Orioles lost. The harassed Barnie thereupon hired the Westminster star, Edward Greer. The Orioles, as old pros, were rebellious. Casey was one of several players accused of clowning on the field in protest. Star pitcher Bob Emslie, fired for his part in it, in time was able to tell Barnie off, as an umpire. Casey, likewise let go, went home, married, and reared seven children. The Orioles, with Greer in centerfield and batting .199, plopped back into the cellar.[21]

When was *the* game played in which Dennis Casey struck out? Bready reported that "research so far has not yet quite fastened upon the specific game." He did, however, throw out one possibility. In a match between the Orioles and the New York Metropolitans, "the game was not decided until the last man, Casey, had been retired . . . in the ninth inning." Yet the final score of this game was 3–2, and it was played in New York, which cast a cloud over its authenticity. Years later one of Dennis's children, Mrs. J. Henry Hipskind who lived in Fort Wayne, Indiana, told Bready quite flatly, "It was my father about whom the poem was written; I feel sure of it."[22] To clinch the case for Dennis, Bready pointed out that Baltimore had to be the locale of "Mighty Casey's" feat. Since that city nurtured the greatest slugger of the twentieth century, "Babe" Ruth, it logically must be the home base for the greatest slugger of the nineteenth century as well.[23]

It was urged by a number of people that Mike "King" Kelly was the real prototype for "Casey." He was Irish, at the peak of his career with Boston when the poem was published, and Thayer was from Massachusetts. While Kelly's baseball credentials were not as impressive as some of his contemporaries', he was probably the most colorful and talented player of his time. His lifetime batting average was only .307, but he hit over .300 eight times in his sixteen-year career and led the National League twice, with marks of .354 in 1884 and .384 in 1886, both with Chicago. Stolen bases were not recorded until Kelly was in his tenth season, but he still stole 325 bases, including 84 for Boston in 116 games in 1887. His base-stealing feats and famous slide were immortalized in song, verse, and movie.[24]

Kelly, who stood five feet ten inches tall and weighed 180 pounds, was not big by classic "Casey" standards, and he was not a noted slugger, although he hit sixty-nine dead-ball home runs during his career. But he was handsome, smart, and had an instinctive flair for the dramatic. "So many stories were told about him," wrote Gardner, "that it is hard to separate truth from myth."[25] Aside from his on-the-field histrionics and heroics, he was a born actor and frequently performed on the stage in the off-season. Although he succumbed to alcoholism and died at an old thirty-seven, in his last years Kelly was well known for his barroom renditions of "Casey at the Bat." He recited it on the stage of the Bijou Theater in Paterson, New Jersey, only a few days before he died on November 8, 1894.[26]

Given a character like Kelly in his prime, it was understandable that an adoring public, particularly in the environs of Boston, identified "Casey" with Kelly and Kelly with "Casey." It will be recalled that Kelly was George D'Vys's hero. When the *Sporting Times* published the last eight stanzas of "Casey" in

July 1888, it substituted "Kelly" for "Casey." Sportswriter Frank Payne and Si Goodfriend insisted Kelly was "Casey."[27] Charles O. Kennedy recalled that "when Ernest Lawrence Thayer wrote this ballad there was much speculation as to which ballplayer he was alluding to. We Boston boys were resentful, thinking he meant Mike 'King' Kelly, the $10,000 Beauty of the Bostons, the highest-priced player up to that time."[28] A number of Kelly poems and the Boston setting for several "Casey" poems further attest to the tendency.

Who did Ernest Thayer really have in mind as the model for his "Casey?" What did he himself say about the mystery? When O. Robinson Casey advanced his claim, the *Syracuse Post-Standard* in Robinson's home town wrote Thayer and inquired if this contention had any basis in fact. Thayer replied as follows:

The poem has no basis in fact. The only Casey actually involved, I am sure about him, was not a ballplayer. He was a big, dour, Irish lad of my high school days. While in high school, I composed and printed myself a very tiny sheet, less than two inches by three. In one issue, I ventured to gag, as we used to say, this Casey boy. He didn't like it and he told me so, and, while he discoursed, his big, clenched, red hands were white at the knuckles. This Casey's name never again appeared in the *Monohippic Gazette*. But I suspect, the incident, many years after, suggested the title for the poem. It was a taunt thrown to the winds. God grant he never catches me.[29]

Many years before the above letter to the Syracuse paper, Thayer told writer Homer Croy something about what he was trying to achieve when he composed the poem.

I evolved "Casey" from the situation I had seen so often in baseball—a crack batsman coming to the bat with the bases filled, and then fallen down. Everybody well knows what immense excitement there is when that situation occurs in baseball, especially when one of the best batsmen of the team comes up. The enthusiasm is at fever heat and if the batsman makes good the crowd goes wild; while, if the batsman strikes out as Casey did, the reverse is the case and the silence that prevails is almost appalling. . . .[30]

What did Mighty "Casey" look like? One with his reputation should certainly be something special. At least a dozen representations of the baseball immortal have appeared in books, newspapers, magazines, and bottles. Since the movie performers of "Casey"—De Wolf Hopper and Wallace Beery—were mere mortals, they must be dismissed out of hand. No mere mortal was "Casey!"

Probably the most attractive portrayal of "Casey at the Bat" is in the panoramic painting by Paul Nonnast. Beneath sunny, blue skies, and before an expectant, well-dressed, well-behaved audience, "Casey" is appreciatively tipping his hat. The angle, from behind the Mudville bench along the third base line, shows a fine view of the first base bleachers, above which rises the American flag, and beyond which lies a small forest of trees. However, the observer is so far removed from home plate that "Casey's" features are unclear. He looks sturdy enough, has dark hair, but no visible moustache.[31]

The most picturesque full-size close-up of "Casey" is in a painting by Albert Dorne. The muscular, rugged batsman has just completed his famous miss. The ball is not yet in the catcher's glove, which suggests that the pitch may have been a change-up and that "Casey" was out ahead with his swing. The batter has a handlebar moustache and, it seems, something of a paunch.[32] In the best book of "Casey" drawings—an attractive, large, twenty-eight-page hardback published by Prentice-Hall and illustrated by Paul Frame—"Casey" is long, lean, muscular, and arrogant. His handlebar moustache, long sideburns, and hair which runs down the nape of the neck are wavy and black.[33]

Several other representations of "Casey," both before and after the swing, show the slugger sporting moustaches of varying shapes and lengths. *Stockton Record* and Adirondack Bat Company advertisements have a grimacing "Casey" finishing his stroke with his feet all tangled up. *The Pittsburgh Press* family magazine presents its less-than-menacing cover "Casey" with a moustache, a badly receding hairline, and a rather rotund, middle-aged appearance. On a colorful, unidentified placemat, the red-headed, red-moustachioed, pot-bellied "Casey" puffs a cigar as he is poised to strike the blow. Cartoonist Gene Mack, at a time when baseball teams were experimenting with exotic clothing styles, presented a Herculean "Casey" attired in frilly briefs. He commented:

There was ease in Casey's manner as he stepped into his place,
There was pride in Casey's bearing and his panties dripped with lace.[34]

Yet despite all the moustaches, the most elaborate portrayals of "Casey" tell us that he was clean-shaven. One of these is in a Walt Disney production, where our hero has a tremendous chest, practically no waistline, and flaming red hair. *Sports Illustrated* published a cartoon dramatization of "Casey" in the spring of 1956, in which the massive batsman looks like a defensive tackle in football, with a neck as thick as Merlin Olsen's. His heavy jaw juts forward, but there is a flicker of a smile as he prepares for the pitch. He has no beard, moustache, or sideburns. In a delightful fifty-six-page large-size cartoon booklet put out by Dover Publications, "Casey" resembles the *Sports Illustrated* "Casey" to a degree, although the jaw is less pronounced. He is clean-shaven and could possibly, when doffing his hat, be bald as well.[35]

In a 1901 pamphlet, perhaps the first independent printing of "Casey at the Bat," our hero is a far cry from the muscular brute so far described. Apparently "Casey" got bigger and tougher as the years passed by. In this early portrayal he looks little more than a boy barely old enough to grow a beard. He is slim, short, and unimpressive. In his great swing, he seems to blow all the air out of the ball park, but he just does not look like "Mighty Casey."[36]

In all of the pictorial representations noted above, "Casey" is batting right-handed. However, a whiskey bottle in the Ezra Brooks Distillery Heritage series released in 1973 has "Casey" batting from the left side. No doubt exists as to the subject's identity; the hitter is rugged and muscular, has a handlebar moustache and long sideburns, and there is an "M" on both his shirt and cap. It is "Casey" all right, but why is he batting left-handed? It has been suggested that he was a switch-hitter, but no evidence anywhere can be educed to support this view. Or perhaps, in another opinion, the bottle designer did not know his left hand from his right.

Darrell Berrigan, who argued persuasively that Mudville was really Stockton, California, and that the "real Casey" played in the California League, pondered the image of our hero:

His face is as illusive as Paul Bunyan's or Shanghai Lil's. Was he, as some have said, a "generalization?" Or was he a Casey who played on some obscure team in one of the smaller California towns. . . . Or was he Michael Kelly, Ten thousand dollar Mike. . . . Looking back over . . . [the] . . . years of dust and memory we can see him, however vaguely, a man of destiny, and conscious of it, leaning on a bat, waiting for the stars to move.[37]

4.

Where Was Mudville?

At 7:15 P.M. on the evening of Friday, August 29, 1952, the lights at Billy Hebert Field in Stockton, California, were dimmed. A bright beam focused on the centerfield scoreboard; the score read 4–2. Over the loudspeaker came the famous words "The outlook wasn't brilliant for the Mudville nine that day. . . ." As the narrator intoned the line, "And when the dust had lifted and they saw what had occurred," the lights gradually came back on. There before the eyes of the assembled throng was Blake, played by Eddie Mulligan, former major league infielder and now president of the Sacramento Club of the Pacific Coast League, "safe at second," and Flynn, represented by Bobby Doerr, the old Boston second baseman, "a-hugging third." "Grinding the ball into his hip" out on the mound, assuming the role of the villain of the piece, was Monte Pearson, former Cleveland and New York Yankee pitcher and author of a no-hitter. And with everyone watching closely, "Mighty Casey"—Max Baer, former heavyweight boxing champion of the world—took his place. The "Great One" took the first two pitches, both called strikes, with equanimity. "Now the pitcher has the ball, and now he lets it go." Max Baer swung with a mighty swing and the deed was done.[1]

The most famous of all reenactments of *the* event was staged in Stockton because of a developing theory that Stockton was indeed *the* Mudville which Thayer used as his model when composing his epic. A number of distinguished personalities were present, and several special events were staged. Albert "Happy" Chandler, lately deposed commissioner of baseball, who was in San Francisco on his way to Japan, stopped off to observe the festivities. Charles Graham, president of the Pacific Coast League, and other notables from that organization were also present. Fred Pearl, Sacramento fight promoter and former baseball announcer, used a megaphone as in days gone by to show the spectators how announcements used to be made. All employees at the ball park were garbed in the dress of that day; the men wore moustaches. Ellsworth "Babe" Dahlgren, most famous for having been Lou Gehrig's successor, now a Hollywood songwriter, introduced his latest number, "What's Left?" A few old-time ballplayers from the Stockton area were seated in a special section and officially recognized during the proceedings. A couple of ancient umpires were on hand and similarly honored. In the regular California League game that night between Stockton and San Jose, the local team wore specially designed nineteenth-century uniforms, with "Mudville" inscribed across the front of the shirt.[2]

Many baseball cities have "bat days," but Stockton is the only place to have "Casey at the Bat" days. The custom began in 1952 at the height of interest over Stockton's Mudville claim and continued for several years. The second reenactment took place June 12, 1953, when the Stockton Ports were hosting the Modesto Reds. This was a special "3-D"—three dimension—night, designed to appeal to sports fans of many types. The first event, commencing at seven o'clock, was a world lightweight championship boxing match between Jimmy Carter and George Aranjo. After the fight came the "Casey" reincarnation, and the final affair of the evening was the regularly scheduled California League game.[3]

For the second reenactment Max Baer again played "Casey"; Guy Fletcher, the Modesto manager and former professional player, was the pitcher; Jerry Donovan, California League president, was the catcher; while "Deacon" Jones, a Yankee scout, Bill Marshall, a Milwaukee scout, Bill Brenzel, a Giant scout, and Charles Walgren, a Red Sox scout, filled the other important parts. Jack Powell, a veteran Pacific Coast League umpire, was the man in blue. Old-time ballplayers were again special guests of the club, and after the game they were entertained at a "hot stove" session by local boosters.[4]

In 1954, as the third reenactment approached, a certain weariness began to set in. After all, if you had seen "Casey" strike out once, or even twice, that ought to be sufficient. And anyhow, there seemed to be a built-in artificiality about reenacting history. To enliven the proceedings in 1954, a number of new wrinkles were added. The Stockton branches of the Native Sons of the Golden West and the Native Daughters of the Golden West were in charge of the program. It was decided to employ a masked batsman for "Casey" and not to reveal his identity until after the strikeout. Any fan who correctly guessed the name of the mystery batsman was to receive free box seat tickets to future Stockton games.[5]

The date selected for the third reenactment was Sunday, June 6, and the scene was to be staged between games of a Stockton-Salinas double-header. The program began with the presentation of a California Bear Flag to the Stockton Club by a trustee of the Native Sons. A barbershop quartet then sang several songs of the eighties-nineties era. Jimmy Longe explained Stockton's Mudville claim over the public address system. Finally a Native Son recited "Casey at the Bat" as the scene was played out on the field.[6]

It was reported that since so much interest had developed over the "Casey" question a major newsreel company planned to film the reenactment and show it in theaters across the country. Furthermore, a "national weekly magazine" was going to carry a story about Stockton and its Mudville claim in an upcoming issue.[7] To add further zest to the affair, prizes were offered to the couple wearing the best old-time costumes. The Modesto Horseless Carriage Club sponsored a parade of old automobiles around the inside of the park. Old-time ballplayers were again honored guests, and two of them served as Flynn and Blake. Jerry Donovan, league president, caught again, and Gil Stratton, west coast announcer, took the umpire's part.[8]

The 1954 reenactment proved a great success, largely because Stockton won the double-header from Salinas. Between the games a masked man wearing an old "Mudville" uniform stepped to the plate and after sneering through his mask, struck out. The mystery man was Warren "Sandy" Sandal, a former Stockton pitcher, who took a brief holiday from his plastering business in Los Angeles to participate in the ceremonies. His identity, however, was a poorly kept secret, and most of the 1,771 fans in attendance knew who he was well before he came to bat.[9] The club must have given away a good many box seat tickets after the game.

The fourth reenactment on Saturday, June 11, 1955, featured "Lefty" Gomez—without disguise—as "Casey." To make sure the whacky southpaw would know what to do and not improvise a spontaneous illogicality, he was carefully briefed on the afternoon of the game. The late Lionel Barrymore's recitation of the poem, used to instruct Gomez, was played during the reenactment. "Lefty" learned his lesson well and quite correctly struck out on three pitches.[10]

Other features of the fourth reenactment were similar to earlier ones. Barbershop harmony music began the program, a parade of "horseless carriages" followed, and prizes were awarded for the best old-style costumes. Ticket-sellers and ticket-takers were garbed in derby hats and the contemporary dress of the eighties and nineties. The Stockton players wore their "Mudville" uniforms in the league game with Modesto, which followed the "mighty miss."[11]

Despite Stockton's great interest in "Casey at the Bat" days during the 1950s, enthusiasm gradually subsided. A 1960 report said that the annual game would be resumed that year, suggesting that it had not been held for quite a while. In a letter to the author in the summer of 1972, the reference librarian of the Stockton Public Library wrote, "We have not had a 'Casey at the Bat' day for some time now—some 15 years or so."[12]

Although interest in the subject waned with the years, Stockton continues to insist it is the original Mudville. What is the basis for this claim? The argument was best set forth in *The Saturday Evening Post* article by Darrell Berrigan. Berrigan cited four factors in support of the theory. (1) Thayer was in San Francisco in 1887–1888 and could have seen a California League game which might have supplied the inspiration for the poem; that he wrote the verse in the East was irrelevant. Furthermore, it was published in the *San Francisco Examiner*, which suggested that Thayer probably had a west coast audience, one familiar with the episode, in mind when he wrote the poem.[13] (2) The Stockton team in 1888 included players named Flynn and Blake. Other names used by

Thayer, Cooney and Barrows, were names of players who performed in the California League in the 1880s, although not with Stockton.[14] (3) Berrigan asserted, without supporting evidence, that Thayer wrote a later poem, "The Man Who Fanned Casey," in which he identified the pitcher who struck out "Casey" as Charlie Sweeney, a mainstay on the Stockton pitching staff in 1887 and 1888. Thus in the matter of names Thayer selected a number of real life California League players to serve his purpose. He would never have done this had he intended some midwestern or eastern city to be Mudville.[15] (4) Stockton for many years *was* known as "Mudville." This term was always a source of embarrassment to the city fathers, which may help explain why they waited so long before claiming that Stockton was *the* Mudville. More frequently it was called "Slough City." Berrigan explained how these terms originated.

Then, as today, it was an important port . . . a base for supplies to the gold mines in the southern Sierras and for the agricultural utopias that sprang up in the San Joaquin Valley when the gold fever abated. The big paddle-wheelers fed the city and carried away its treasures. They chunked out of San Francisco and up the Sacramento and San Joaquin, settling down at last alongside Banner Island. Often they stuck there for days, waiting for the tide to lift them out of the ooze. The captains had grounds for dubbing Stockton Mudville.[16]

The old ballfield used by the Stockton club in the 1880s was located on Banner Island in the San Joaquin River. When the "Casey" claim became a live issue in the city, amateur archaeologists conducted excavations on Banner Island hoping to discover documentary proof for their cause. All they found, however, were rusty razor blades and dirty overalls, none of which, Berrigan noted, "could be traced to Casey." Berrigan believed they dug in the wrong place and should have concentrated on a filled-in waterway at the northern end of the island. In the old days a line of houseboats, known as "arks," was kept anchored at that point. Gambling, drinking, and other sinful pastimes were practiced constantly on the arks and the ballplayers were no doubt good customers. Berrigan speculated that if "Casey dropped any relic about—a medal, or a rabbit's foot or an engraved flask—he most probably did it there."[17]

Did Thayer have in mind any particular game played at Stockton? Yes, he did, although there is a small conflict of opinion among local historians on the subject. One school argued that the game took place in 1888 between Stockton and a team of major league all-stars just returning from a world tour. This, of course, referred to Albert G. Spalding's collection of famous players who left San Francisco in the fall of 1888 and, after circumnavigating the globe, arrived in New York in the spring of 1889. The other school insisted that the game, played in the spring of 1888, matched Stockton and a group of big league players who had wintered in California.[18]

Thayer had been in California, and the names he used in his poem were names of actual players whom he might have seen. What was more logical than to conclude that these people, and this setting, were models for "Casey at the

Bat." That no one named "Casey" played there at the time could be easily explained. Thayer simply preferred not to embarrass any individual. And Stockton certainly was called "Mudville." No one had ever bragged about this before, but it had now become a point of pride and a keystone in the theory. However, the Stockton claim had a number of flaws.

In fact, even certain Stockton writers were not convinced of their community's claim. An editorial in the *Stockton Record* at the time of the first reenactment in 1952 observed that, "Of late there has been found reason to identify Stockton of actuality with Mudville of legend. There is no definite link, mind you, but. . . . " The following year on the eve of the second replay, the same paper conceded, "little fact supports the legend that Stockton truly is the 'Mudville' of the epic written in San Francisco." [19] In other news accounts it was stated that even though no absolute proof could be advanced for the Stockton claim, could any city advance a better one?

These misgivings were justified. For one thing, there was the problem of the game. Both schools of thought were in error on this point. Stockton could not have played Spalding's major league all-stars at all because they never reached Calfornia until October 1888, four months after the poem was published. The other theory, that Stockton played a crowd of major leaguers in the spring of 1888 who had wintered in California, was equally erroneous because Thayer returned to Massachusetts early in February 1888, before the exhibition season began.

It was asserted that Thayer in a later poem, "The Man Who Fanned Casey," identified the pitcher who struck out "Casey" as Charles Sweeney, a Stockton pitcher. The thorough research by "Casey" scholar Martin Gardner, however, has uncovered no second "Casey" poem by Thayer. "I'm sure," Gardner wrote, "that if Thayer ever wrote another Casey ballad, we'd know about it." [20]

One Stockton apologist, Joanne Mary Ghio, submitted that *the* game was between the major league all-stars "returning from a world tour early in 1888," that John Patrick Parnell Cahill played with the all-stars in that game, that Sweeney pitched for Stockton, and that Stockton won, 4–2. Not content with this list of errors and improbabilities, she proceeded to confuse the situation even more. If Sweeney fanned "Casey" (Cahill), she noted, "it would then not be likely that Mudville would have been saddened since Sweeney performed for the home team." Undeterred by this, however, she continued: "Contemporary newspaper reports indicated that after the game there was general rioting in the grandstand. It is possible that bets had been placed on individual performers, thus the disappointment of Casey's sad showing would have spread gloom throughout the crowd." [21]

This was too much and even Joanne Mary Ghio herself recognized it. She concluded by speculating that perhaps Thayer did not intend to report exactly what happened in that game, but only to use it as a basis. He utilized the main points and developed them for his own purpose. [22] Of course, the fundamental weakness in this theory again is that the major league all-stars did not return from their world tour early in 1888. They returned early in 1889, almost a year after the poem was published, and when they did return, it was to New York, not California.[23]

Martin Gardner asserted unhesitatingly that Mudville was located in eastern Kansas. In his *Annotated Casey at the Bat* he wrote that "Mudville was a farming village near the east border of Anderson County, Kansas, about 60 miles southeast of Topeka. It was on the south bank of Polecat Creek, seven miles west of where Centerville,[24] in Linn County, is still located. Neither Mudville nor the creek exist today."[25] Mudville and Centerville may be found on the map which is printed in the endpapers of *The Annotated Casey*.

In some verses, Centerville is referred to as Frogtown because, according to Gardner, the croaking bullfrogs in nearby Bugville Swamp made such a racket that they could be heard in Mudville. Among the other towns mentioned in "Casey" literature, Slamtown (also in Linn County) is about fifteen miles northeast of Mudville and eleven miles due south of Centerville.[26] Midvale, nonexistent now, was twenty miles south of Mudville on the Anderson County line.

While no one has as yet challenged Gardner's Kansas-Mudville claim, it should be pointed out that no one from eastern Kansas has come forth to support it. It could be, of course, that Gardner, a known jokester, was simply having some fun and invented the Kansas story. His argument, on the other hand, does not lack force and, when accompanied by a map, demands serious consideration. An examination of a modern map of Kansas reveals the town of Centerville in the west central section of Linn County, while a short distance away in Anderson County is the village of Bush City, which sounds suspiciously like Mudville.

The only other Mudville claims originated with the discredited George D'Vys and Dan Casey. In his affidavit to Harry Peck, D'Vys asserted that the area of suburban Boston in which he grew up and from which he got his inspiration to "write" the last eight stanzas of "Casey" was called Mudville. In his radio broadcast, Dan Casey said that the section around the old Philadelphia ball park also was called Mudville. D'Vys and Dan Casey were probably right on this point, but were they speaking of the "real" Mudville? We cannot be sure. Without more conclusive evidence the location of Thayer's Mudville must remain as elusive as "Casey" himself.

Dan Casey, the old-time pitcher and most insistent claimant to have been the "original Casey."

"Mighty Casey" as he appears on an old place-mat

"Mighty Casey" striking out, from a 1901 printing of the poem

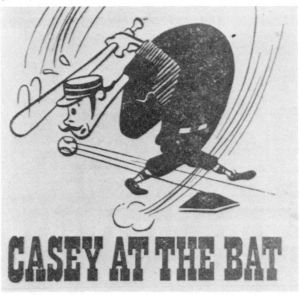

"Mighty Casey" striking out in an Adirondack Bat advertisement

"Mighty Casey" in frilly lace

An Ezra Brooks bottle showing "Mighty Casey" poised to swing

An old-time recording of "Casey at the Bat" could be heard for a nickel

Digby Bell's reply to "Casey at the Bat"

Casey has been famed long enough for his immortal fanning act. Mr. Bell thinks the man who did the trick, the redoubtable twirler of the Frogtown team, should have his share of the glory; and he gives it to him in this witty take-off,

"The Man Who Fanned Casey"

An advertisement for Digby Bell's recording of "The Man Who Fanned Casey"

A comic "Casey" in the author's possession

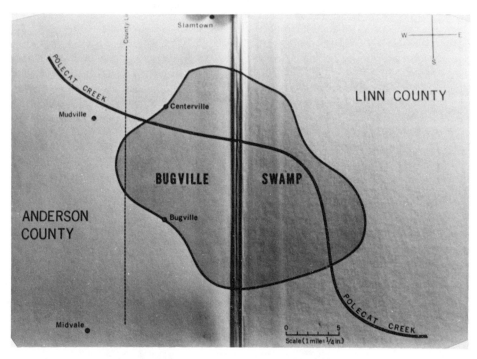

A map of eastern Kansas showing Mudville's location. Reprinted from Martin Gardner, *The Annotated Casey at the Bat.*

PART TWO
THE LITERARY RECORD

When Ernest L. Thayer casually launched "Casey" into immortality, he not only invited heated controversies over authorship, protagonist, and geography, he did much more. He founded a literary genus, which might be labeled "Casius Extrapolatus." From the seedling of "Casey at the Bat" have flowered innumerable additional verses dealing with such subjects as the pitcher who struck out "Casey," "Casey's" redemption, and the feats and failures of "Casey's" family and relations. There are poems setting forth further deeds and misdeeds of "Casey," parodies geared to "Casey at the Bat," and verses with only casual "Casey" references but which would not have been written had it not been for "Casey at the Bat." There has been an ethnic "Casey" and a "mod Casey." There have been verses about Mudville's history, a poem concerning Hopper, and most impressive of all, a "Casey" opera.

The literary record of "Casey at the Bat" is not easy to sort out. Most confusing is the total absence of consistency or logic among the "Casey" poems. Were a writer to attempt to put together a biography based on the poems about "Casey," as some have done with the stories about Sherlock Holmes, he would face far more serious problems than Sherlockian scholars ever confronted. Different names are used for the opposing pitcher and for other characters in the story. The names of towns are manufactured, abandoned, and resurrected indiscriminately. Absurdities, anachronisms, and contradictions abound. It is obvious that when a new writer decided to compose a "Casey" poem he paid scant heed to what had gone before, if indeed he was aware of anything that had gone before.

In this section of the book no attempt is made to iron out the many wrinkles. Rather, the poems are grouped topically, and an introductory note prefaces each topic as well as each poem. If no coherent record can be established, at least the wide range of ''Casey'' literature can be brought together in one place.

5.

The Pitcher

The first problem facing anyone attempting an analysis of the "Casey" literature is the identity of the opposing pitcher. Who was this forgotten wizard who struck "Mighty Casey" out? Thayer was of no help, having given no name to the man. There have been four poems about the pitcher, two related poems explaining why "Casey" missed, and two discussions of the strategy employed by both teams on that momentous pitch.

In the four poems the pitcher has four different names. Chronologically, he is known as Hagen, Flannigan, Riley, and Snedeker, but the last of the four has been accepted by Martin Gardner as the correct one. Snedeker appeared for the first time, not in any poem, but in the 1953 opera *The Mighty Casey*. Working backward from this point, Gardner concluded that the early poems were in error in identifying the pitcher. One exception to this was Riley, because Riley was really Snedeker. You see, as Gardner explained, "when he left Centerville to pitch for the Boston Beaneaters, he changed his last name from Snedeker to Riley, his middle name and his mother's maiden name."[1] Thus the two Riley poems are really about James Riley "Fireball" Snedeker.

The first pitcher poem, "The Man Who Fanned Casey," appeared as early as 1909 on a phonograph record and was recited by Digby Bell, who, like Hopper, was "a popular singing comedian of the day." In the following version, taken from Gardner's *Annotated Casey*, the pitcher's name was originally Hagen, but Gardner changed it in view of his later information.[2]

THE MAN WHO FANNED CASEY

Anonymous—1909

I'm just an ordinary fan, and I don't count for much,
But I'm for writing history with a true and honest touch;
It isn't often that I knock—I'll put you next to that—
But I must interpose a word on *Casey at the Bat.*

Oh, yes, I must admit it, the poem is a beaut,
Been runnin' through my thinker since our team got on the chute;
I heard an actor fan recite it thirteen years ago,
He sort of introduced it in the progress of the show.

It made a hit from gallery, down to the parquet floor,
But now I've got to thinking, and that poem makes me sore;
I'd like to know why any fan should be so off his nut,
About the Mighty Casey who proved himself a mutt.

The score, we're told, stood four to two, one inning left to play,
The Frogtown twirler thought he had things pretty much his way;
So in the ninth, with two men down, he loosened up a bit,
And Flynn scratched out a single, Blake let loose a two-base hit.

Then from the stand and bleachers there arose a mighty roar,
They wanted just that little hit they knew would tie the score;
And there at bat was Casey, Mighty Casey, Mudville's pride,
But was the Frogtown slabster sent balloonin', terrified?

Now in the ninth, with two men down and Casey at the bat,
Most pitchers would have let him walk—we all are sure of that;
But Fireball was a hero, he was made of sterner stuff,
It's *his* kind get the medals and the long newspaper puff.

He knew the time had come for him to play a winning role,
He heard the fans a-yelling, it was music to his soul;
He saw the gleam of confidence in Mighty Casey's eye,
"I'll strike him out!" Fireball resolved, "I'll do it or I'll die!"

He stood alone and friendless in that wild and frenzied throng,
There wasn't even one kind word to boost his game along;
But back in Frogtown where they got the plays by special wire,
The fans stood ready, if he won, to set the town on fire.

Now Fireball twirls his body on the truest corkscrew plan,
And hurls a swift inshoot that cuts the corner of the pan;
But Casey thought the first ball pitched would surely be a ball,
And didn't try to strike it, to the great disgust of all.

Again the Frogtown twirler figures dope on Mudville's pride,
And Casey thinks the next will be an outshoot breaking wide;
But Fireball shot a straight one down the middle of the plate,
And Casey waited for a curve until it was too late.

And now the mighty slugger is a-hangin' on the string,
If another good one comes along, it's up to him to swing;
The jaunty smile, Fireball observed, has faded from his face,
And a look of straining agony is there to take its place.

One moment Fireball pauses, hides the ball behind his glove,
And then he drives it from him with a sweeping long arm shove;
And now the air is shattered, and the ball's in Thatcher's mitt,
For Casey, Mighty Casey, hadn't figured on the spit![3]

The second pitcher poem was about a man named Flannigan. Actually, the poem was more about "Casey's" revenge than the pitcher's exploits, but because it dealt with the man who struck out "Casey" it is included here. It will be quickly noted that Flannigan was not much of a pitcher after all.

HIS NAME WAS FLANNIGAN

by Frank Perry—1925

You've heard of Mighty Casey, who missed three o'er the pan,
But I'm not thinking of him so much, as the guy who made him fan;
This pitcher's name was Flannigan, he had nothing much but crust,
And outside of that Casey episode, he was an awful bust.

His curve ball gave us all a laugh, it broke behind the plate,
And his fast one—when he got it going—was twenty seconds late;
Of all the bushers I have seen, his head was swelled the worst,
And when he set this Casey down, we thought that he would burst.

He told Mike Dunn, our manager, it was fierce to hear him gloat,
"I'll stop dat bunch each time I start, I've got dis Casey's goat;"
When Mudville hit our town next trip, 'twas Flannigan's turn to work,
And the hand he got as he strode to the box, made him strut and pose and smirk.

Of all the games of ball I've played, and I'm still sticking yet,
That game with Mudville in our town, is the one I can't forget;
The first one Casey hit rolled off a roof across the street,
The next one cleared the right field wall by easy forty feet.

The third time that he came to bat, he spat upon his hands,
And bounced one off my legs at third that landed in the stands;
The fourth time Casey took his place, the crowd stood up to shout,
But Flannigan would not walk him, he said, "I'll strike him out!"

"Dis Casey's full of horseshoes, he's got nuttin' else but luck,"
Then Casey smacked the first one and Flannigan tried to duck;
When Casey started for the bag, the umpire hollered, "Out!"
Then Casey stopped and tore for him, and how that guy could clout.

"I don't mean you," the umpire yelled, "it's Flannigan, because,
You crashed him on the jaw that time," and out he surely was;
I talked to Flannigan that night, that bird was feeling tough,
And he pulled that famous alibi, "I didn't have my stuff."[4]

Riley-Snedeker appeared in the following two poems, which are recited in the first person. They reflect the pitcher's torment at being consistently over-looked in the general ado about "Casey's" miss. After all, the pitcher should have gotten some credit.

RILEY IN THE BOX

Anonymous—no date

There's been a lot of smoking over Casey and his bat,
And how he didn't win the game and other guff like that;
They've made some rhymes about him and that sort of swelled his fame,
But what's the good of crackin' up the mutt that lost the game?

I'd heard about this Casey and the way he smashed 'em out,
I'd heard about his posing just to hear the bleachers shout;
So when we tackled Casey's team you may be sure I tried,
To put a kink in Casey's game and puncture Casey's pride.

For those of you who seen the game it's easy to recall,
That we'd have lost and they'd have won had Casey hit the ball;
'Twas in the ninth with bases full that Casey came to bat,
And Lordy, how the bleachers cheered when on his hands he spat.

I doubled up and than unkinked and let the horsehide fly,
But Casey only stood and smiled and watched the ball go by;
"One strike!" the umpire shouted, and I thought there'd be a fight,
But Casey sort of turned and said, "Be quiet, lads, he's right."

Again I shot a screamer, and it whistled o'er the plate,
If Casey thought he'd strike at it, he thought a bit too late;
"Two strikes!" the umpire bellowed, but the bleachers didn't shout,
I looked at Casey and I saw his smile was dying out.

I braced myself and sent him one in my peecoolyer style,
And Casey swang with all his might—and missed it by a mile!
No matter what the po-try says of Casey and his bat,
This is the way it happened, you can lay your coin on that.

The bands are playing somewhere, but 'tis not in Casey's town,
They're serenading Riley, he's the man who put him down;
And "no skiddoo" for Casey's fame, his number's "twenty-three!"
'Twas Riley, Pitcher Riley, was the hero, don't you see?[5]

RILEY ON THE MOUND

Anonymous—No Date

I don't suppose you've heard of me, there ain't much doubt of that,
But I'm the guy who made 'em write about *Casey at the Bat*;
I was on the mound that day, when poor Casey met his doom,
I turned happy Mudville town into a state of deep gloom.

I remember the big game very well, we were leadin' four-to-two,
Git 'em out just one more time, that's all I had to do;
The roar that went up from the grandstand could be heard for twenty miles,
Five thousand fans stark ravin' mad, their faces covered with smiles.

I knowed what it was set 'em off, their hero was comin' to bat,
Ol' Mighty Casey was strollin' to the plate, but I could sure take care of that;
He tipped his cap and waved his hand and that made the fans more wild,
But it didn't bother me one little bit, I just stood there and smiled.

I put me fast one just inside and Casey let it go by,
"Strike One!" the umpire screamed, and Casey didn't bat an eye;
When the umpire called next "Strike Two," I thought they'd chase him outa town,
And it looked as though they might've too, if ol' "Case" hadn't calmed them down.

The pressure was gettin' to us both by now, so I pulled me belt up a hitch,
Then reared back me good right arm for me number one "Sunday pitch";
Casey swung with all his might, he really gave it all he had,
And even though I struck 'im out, I couldn't help feelin' kinda sad.

Sure we won the pennant, but when I looked at the crowd,
They'd turned their backs on Mighty Casey as he walked away, head bowed;
Now all this took place many years ago, and ever since though we've read,
About poor ol' Casey strikin' out, it should've been 'bout me instead.

So when you guys are sittin' around, jawin' about our favorite game,
Remember Casey if that's your wish, but it was RILEY put 'im to shame.[6]

Two short poems purported to explain why "Casey" missed, although one suggestion on the subject—the spitball—has already been made.

WHY CASEY WHIFFED

by Don Fairbairn—1937

The ball fans always wondered, and in Mudville most of all,
Why the mighty Mr. Casey did not clout that final ball;
Did not poke the old potato into stratospheric space,
When the winning runs were rotting there on third and second base.

Now a cousin of a neighbor of great Casey's furnace man,
Who was there that eve' when he came home to meet the sneering pan
Of his wife, and her six brothers, and a dozen other guys,
Blames the whole thing on a batboy who had bandy-legged eyes.

He was never seen before then, and he vanished with the game,
Like those runts in fairy stories which they tell us did the same;
He had red hair and was toothless and he said his name was "Buck,"
And his every move and action was a-dripping with bad luck.

Casey took the bat he handed, then he felt "all odd" he said,
At the plate the awful vision of those optics filled his head;
Sure, they whiffed him, but he realized as the fans groaned to the skies,
He was hoo-dooed by the urchin with the double-crossing eyes![7]

CASEY AT THE BAT

Anonymous—1948

The sneer is gone from Casey's lips, his teeth are clenched in hate,
He pounds with cruel vengeance his bat upon the plate;
And now the pitcher holds the ball, and now he lets it go,
And now the air is shattered by the force of Casey's blow.

Oh, somewhere in this favored land the sun is shining bright,
The band is playing somewhere, and somewhere hearts are light;
And somewhere men are laughing, and somewhere children shout,
But there is no joy in Boston: Mighty Casey has struck out.

There were no Adirondack Bats, those days beyond recall,
If he'd had an Adirondack—he would'a hit the ball.[8]

Seventy-three years after "Casey" struck out, Leonard Koppett revealed the details of a pressbox discussion among several of the writers on the day following the game. While they were unanimous in their view that Ernest Thayer had missed much of what happened by concentrating on the final inning and that he should have been down in the locker room after the game interviewing "Casey" instead of up in the pressbox writing poetry, their main complaint was against the strategy employed by the two managers. One question was why Barrows, who was hitless in the last twenty-five times at bat, was allowed to hit in the ninth inning. Another question was why the opposing pitcher, whatever his name, deigned to pitch to "Casey" with the tying run on second base. Better to put the winning run on base than give "Casey" the opportunity to drive it in himself.

And why did the pitcher throw an 0-and–2 pitch right down the middle? That is the kind of pitch you automatically waste. This caused an argument because one of the writers swore that the pitch bounced a foot outside the plate. A final question was why "Casey," representing the winning run in the last of the ninth with two outs, took the first two pitches. This prompted another argument between those who said "Casey" was ordered to take the pitches and those who insisted that he was always on his own.[9]

Arthur Robinson also raised several questions on the subject, suggesting that Thayer was not the world's greatest reporter. He did not "even mention the name of either the opposing team or the pitcher. . . . " Moreover, he did not indicate the kind of pitch on which "Casey" struck out. "And why didn't the opposing pitcher give Casey, the greatest of home run hitters, an intentional base on balls? Flynn was on third and Blakey on second and first base was open."[10] When one pauses to ponder the matter, it is surprising that so much attention has always been centered on the strikeout and that it was many years later before anyone thought to question the strategy involved in the final inning of the great game.

6.

Redemption

Following his embarrassing strikeout, Casey was not long in redeeming himself. Beginning as early as 1895, only six years after "Casey at the Bat" appeared, a number of writers have described the comeback of our hero. In nearly all of these ballads Mudville faced the same team and pitcher that it faced on the day of "Casey's" misfortune, although like Thayer, these writers forgot to mention who the team and pitcher were. And in practically every case the reader is rushed through to the bottom of the ninth inning, where there were two out, two or three men on base, and Mudville was trailing by two or three runs. "Casey" came to bat and in almost every poem took the first two pitches for called strikes before whacking the next one for a tape measure home run to win the game. The eleven poems in this chapter—one has two other versions, which are also included—are presented in the order of their publication.

"When Casey Slugged the Ball," composed by Cincinnati writer Nat Wright, first appeared in *Sporting Life*, May 11, 1895, and was reprinted in *The Sporting News*, November 11, 1899. In this ballad Mudville was playing the "Giants," but such details as who was pitching, how many were out, and the inning in which the action took place were omitted.

WHEN CASEY SLUGGED THE BALL

by Nat Wright—1895

Oh, you all have heard of Mudville, heard of mighty Casey too,
Of the groans amid the bleachers as the ball thrice past him flew;
But you haven't heard the story, the best story of them all,
Of the day in happy Mudville, when great Casey slugged the ball.

'Twas the day they played "the Giants," and the score stood ten to eight,
Two men were on the bases, and great Casey at the plate;

"Swipe her, Casey," yelled the rooters and the hero doffed his cap,
Three to win and two to tie and Casey at the bat.

Mid a hush of expectation, now the ball flies past his head,
Great Casey grins a sickly grin, "Strike one," the umpire said;
Again the pitcher raised his arm, again the horsehide flew,
Great Casey spat upon the ground, and the umpire said, "Strike two."

"It's a roast," came from the grandstand, "he is bought without a doubt,"
"He is rotten!" roared the bleachers, "throw the daylight robber out!"
"I'll break your face," says Casey, "that wan wint below me knee,
If I miss the nixt, ye blackguard, Ye won't live long to see."

The next one came like lightning and the umpire held his breath,
For well he knew if Casey missed, 'twould surely mean his death;
But Casey swung to meet it, backed by all his nerve and gall,
Oh, if you had but heard the yell, as Casey smashed the ball!

He caught the pigskin on the nose, it cleared the big town lot,
It sailed above the high church tower, in vain the fielder sought;
And Casey didn't even run, he stopped awhile to talk,
And then amid the deafening cheers, he came round in a walk.

And now he keeps a beer saloon, he is Mayor of the town,
The people flock to see him, from all the country round;
And you need not look for Mudville in the map upon the wall,
Because the town is called Caseyville, since Casey slugged the ball.[1]

The *San Francisco Examiner*, which put Casey "on the blink" in the first
place, made amends for its wrongful act sixteen years later.

CASEY'S NAME REDEEMED

Anonymous—1905

There were thoughts in Casey's thinker when it came his turn to hit,
Half-past five the clock recorded—it was getting time to quit;
Casey felt his belt a-loosening—supper time was drawing near,
"Let him pass me up a good one, and I'll end the fun right here."

Saying this, his feet he planted firmly in the well-packed earth,
"Though the poet says I strike out, here is where I show my worth";
To the plate the ball came sailing—Casey soused it on the beak,
Out it soared toward the palings, leaped the fence and made a sneak.

Round the bases Casey sauntered his home run won the game,
And wiped out a stain which long had been disgraceful to his name.[2]

The greatest feat of redemption occurred in the most famous "other" poem, "Casey's Revenge." Like the original, this verse went through several corrupted and revised versions and experienced a minor dispute over authorship. By majority opinion, the future dean of American sportswriters, Grantland Rice, is considered the author. However, no one has yet discovered the first publication of this piece and only in roundabout fashion has Rice asserted authorship. While the poem is supposed to have been written in 1906, the earliest published version discovered by Martin Gardner appeared in *The Speaker*, June 1907. But already in this printing three of the sixteen stanzas have been omitted and the author was named as "James Wilson." [3]

Rice published "Casey's Revenge" in a bound volume of his own poems, *Baseball Ballads*, in 1910. Soon thereafter, in a revised edition of *The National Game* (1911), Alfred Spink included the poem, attributing it to Rice. Francis Richter published the poem in his *History and Records of Baseball* (1914), also attributing it to Rice. "Casey's Revenge" was later published in two anthologies of verse, both printings of which omitted the third, fourth, and fifth stanzas, and attributed authorship to the mysterious "James Wilson." "James Wilson," Martin Gardner speculated, was "perhaps the pseudonym Rice had previously used." [4]

An unusual assertion has been made that Ernest Thayer himself wrote "Casey's Revenge." One George Poultney, described as a baseball researcher, contended in the *Stockton* (California) *Record* that Thayer wrote the poem and that it was published in the *San Francisco Examiner* about a month after the first poem was published in 1888. Charles O'Brien Kennedy, a veteran actor, stage director, and playwright, picked up from some source, perhaps Poultney, the idea that Thayer was indeed the author and said so when he included "Casey's Revenge" in his 1954 anthology, *A Treasury of American Ballads: Gay, Naughty, and Classic*. Tristram Coffin, writer and folklorist, followed Kennedy in attributing "Casey's Revenge" to Thayer, although with less insistence, in his 1975 *Illustrated Book of Baseball Folklore*. [5]

Two facts dispose of this contention. First, Grantland Rice included "Casey's Revenge" in both anthologies of his poems, *Baseball Ballads* and *Only the Brave*. Dave Camerer also included it in *The Best of Grantland Rice*. Obviously, Rice would not have included the poem in his own collection of verses if he had not written it. But more important, in November 1906, in introducing his poem about "Casey's" failure in football at "Yarvard," Rice made the following observation: "All remember how the mighty Casey lost the famed battle at Mudville by paddling the ozone in the last round of play. *Later on we depicted the artful manner in which he secured his revenge. . . .* " (Italics supplied.) This would appear to be the "proof positive," in lieu of other evidence, that Rice did write "Casey's Revenge," and that he probably wrote it in 1906. [6]

On the basis of internal evidence, the case is almost conclusive that Rice rather than Thayer wrote "Casey's Revenge." The style, the use of baseball slang, and other literary devices are close to the pattern employed by Rice in his many other baseball poems. In addition to all of this, the fact that Thayer himself never made any claim to having written "Casey's Revenge," or ever referred to it in any published communication, should lay to rest the view that it was his work.

The original version of "Casey's Revenge," as it appeared in *Baseball Ballads*, follows.

There were saddened hearts in Mudville for a week or even more,
There were muttered oaths and curses—every fan in town was sore;
"Just think," said one, "how soft it looked with Casey at the bat,
And then to think he'd go and spring a bush league trick like that!"

All his past fame was forgotten—he was now a hopeless "shine,"
They called him "Strike-Out Casey," from the mayor down the line;
And as he came to bat each day his bosom heaved a sigh,
While a look of hopeless fury shone in mighty Casey's eye.

He pondered in the days gone by that he had been their king,
That when he strolled up to the plate they made the welkin ring;
But now his nerve had vanished for when he heard them hoot,
He "fanned" or "popped out" daily, like some minor league recruit.

He soon began to sulk and loaf, his batting eye went lame,
No home runs on the score card now were chalked against his name;
The fans without exception gave the manager no peace,
For one and all kept clamoring for Casey's quick release.

The Mudville squad began to slump, the team was in the air,
Their playing went from bad to worse—nobody seemed to care;
"Back to the woods with Casey!" was the cry from Rooters' Row,
"Get some one who can hit the ball, and let that big dub go!"

The lane is long, some one has said, that never turns again,
And Fate, though fickle, often gives another chance to men;
And Casey smiled, his rugged face no longer wore a frown—
The pitcher who had started all the trouble came to town.

All Mudville had assembled—ten thousand fans had come,
To see the twirler who had put big Casey on the bum;
And when he stepped into the box, the multitude went wild,
He doffed his cap in proud disdain, but Casey only smiled.

"Play Ball!" the umpire's voice rang out, and then the game began,
But in that throng of thousands there was not a single fan
Who thought that Mudville had a chance, and with the setting sun,
Their hopes sank low—the rival team was leading "four to one."

The last half of the ninth came round, with no change in the score,
But when the first man up hit safe, the crowd began to roar;
The din increased, the echo of ten thousand shouts was heard,
When the pitcher hit the second and gave "four balls" to the third.

Three men on base—nobody out—three runs to tie the game!
A triple meant the highest niche in Mudville's hall of fame;
But here the rally ended and the gloom was deep as night,
When the fourth one "fouled to catcher" and the fifth "flew out to right."

A dismal groan in chorus came, a scowl was on each face,
When Casey walked up, bat in hand, and slowly took his place;
His bloodshot eyes in fury gleamed, his teeth were clenched in hate,
He gave his cap a vicious hook and pounded on the plate.

But fame is fleeting as the wind and glory fades away,
There were no wild and woolly cheers, no glad acclaim this day;
They hissed and groaned and hooted as they clamored: "Strike him out!"
But Casey gave no outward sign that he had heard this shout.

The pitcher smiled and cut one loose—across the plate it sped,
Another hiss, another groan, "Strike one!" the umpire said;
Zip! Like a shot the second curve broke just below the knee,
"Strike two!" the umpire roared aloud, but Casey made no plea.

No roasting for the umpire now—his was an easy lot,
But here the pitcher whirled again—was that a rifle shot?
A whack, a crack, and out through the space the leather pellet flew,
A blot against the distant sky, a speck against the blue.

Above the fence in center field in rapid whirling flight,
The sphere sailed on—the blot grew dim and then was lost to sight;
Ten thousand hats were thrown in air, ten thousand threw a fit,
But no one ever found the ball that mighty Casey hit.

O, somewhere in this favored land dark clouds may hide the sun,
And somewhere bands no longer play and children have no fun!
And somewhere over blighted lives there hangs a heavy pall,
But Mudville hearts are happy now, for Casey hit the ball.[7]

Both revisions of "Casey's Revenge" have only a few word changes. The plot unfolds exactly the same way. No date is given for the first revision, published in *Only the Brave*. The mention of Babe Ruth indicates it was after 1920.

There were broken hearts in Mudville for a week or even more,
There were muttered, throbbing curses—every fan in town was sore;

"Just think" said one, "how soft it looked with Casey at the bat—
And then to think he'd go and spring a bush-league trick like that."

All his past fame was forgotten—he was now a hopeless punk,
They called him "Strike-out Casey"—both the sober and the drunk;
And as he came to bat each day his stout lungs heaved a sigh,
While a look of hopeless fury shone in mighty Casey's eye.

He pondered on the days gone by that he had been their king—
That when he strolled up to the plate they made the welkin ring;
Their echoes socked the mountainside and rolled across the flat,
As Casey—mighty Casey—swaggered Ruth-like up to bat.

He soon began to sulk and loaf—his batting eye went lame,
No home runs on the score card now were chalked against his name;
And the fans without exception gave the manager no peace,
As one and all kept clamoring for Casey's quick release.

The Mudville team began to slump—the clucks were in the air,
Their playing went from bad to worse—nobody seemed to care;
"Back to the bush with Casey!" was the cry from Rooters' Row,
"Get someone who can hit the ball and let that big mug go!"

The sneer was gone from Casey's lips—the smile had left his face,
Defiance, known to vanished days, no longer held its place;
For men are made by deed on deed, by grinding mile on mile,
But men are broken in a flash when Fortune shifts her smile.

The lane is long, someone has said, that never turns again,
And fate, though fickle, often slips another chance to men;
In Casey's eyes a new light shone—his forehead lost its frown—
The pitcher who had fanned him in the pinches came to town.

All Mudville had assembled there—ten thousand fans had come,
To cheer the twirler who had turned their king into a bum;
And when he stepped into the box the raving mob went wild,
He doffed his cap in proud disdain—but Casey only smiled.

"Play Ball"—the umpire's call went out—and then the game began,
But in that mob of sorrow there was not a single fan
Who thought that Mudville had a chance—and with the setting sun,
Their hopes sank low—the rival team was leading four to one.

The last half of the ninth came 'round—with no change in the score,
But when the first man up hit safe the crowd began to roar;
The din increased—the echo of ten thousand throats was heard,
As the wobbling pitcher packed the paths from first around to third.

Three men on base—nobody out—three runs to tie the game!
A triple meant the highest niche in Mudville's hall of fame;
But here the rally ended and the gloom was deep as night,
As the fourth one fouled to catcher and the fifth flew out to right.

A dismal groan in chorus came—a scowl was on each face,
As Casey walked up, bat in hand, and grimly took his place;
His bloodshot eyes in fury gleamed, his teeth were clenched in hate,
He gave his cap a vicious tug and pounded on the plate.

But fame is fleeting as the wind—and glory fades away,
There were no wild and woolly cheers—no glad acclaim this day;
They called for Tony or for Pete—for bat boy or for clown—
For anyone—except the punk who threw their city down.

The pitcher grinned—and cut one loose—across the plate it sped,
Another hiss—another groan—"Strike one," the umpire said;
Zip—like a shot the second curve broke just above his knee—
"Strike two," the umpire called again—but Casey made no plea.

No roasting for the umpire now—his was an easy lot—
But here the pitcher whirled again—was that a rifle shot?
A crash—a smash—and out through space the leather pellet flew,
A blot against the distant sky—a speck against the blue.

Above the fence in center field in rapid whirling flight,
The ball sailed on—the blot grew dim—and then was lost to sight;
Ten thousand hats were thrown in air—ten thousand threw a fit,
But no one ever found the ball that mighty Casey hit.

    L'envoi

There is no sequel to this plot—except in Mudville's square,
The bronze bust of a patriot—arms crossed—is planted there;
His cap is cocked above one eye—and from his rugged face,
The sneer still curls above the crowd—across the marketplace.

And underneath, in solid bronze, these words are graved in flame—
"Here is a man who rose and fell—and rose again to fame—
He blew a big one in the pinch—but facing jeering throngs,
He came through Hell to scramble back—and prove a champ belongs."[8]

In the other revision of "Casey's Revenge," Rice drops the "L'envoi" and substitutes a concluding stanza which shows the motivation behind "Casey's" heroic comeback.

There were saddened hearts in Mudville for a week or even more,
There we muttered oaths and curses, every fan in town was sore;
"Just think," said one, "how soft it looked with Casey at the bat,
And then to think he'd go and spring a bush league trick like that!"

His past fame was forgotten—he was now a cock-eyed bum,
They called him "Strike Out Casey," and they made the welkin hum;
And as he came to bat each day his bosom heaved a sigh,
While a look of hopeless fury shone in mighty Casey's eye.

He pondered in the days gone by that he had been their king,
That when he came to bat each day they waited for his bing;
But now his nerve was shattered, for when he heard their boo,
He fanned or popped out daily like some rookie on a stew.

He soon began to sulk and loaf, his batting eye went lame,
No home runs on the score card now were chalked against his name;
And fans without exception gave the manager no peace,
For one and all kept clamoring for Casey's quick release.

The Mudville squad began to slump—the team was in the air,
Their playing went from bad to worse—nobody seemed to care;
"Back to the bush with Casey!" was the cry from rooter's row,
"Get some one who can hit the ball and let that big mug go!"

The lane is long, some one has said, that never turns again,
And fate though fickle often gives another chance to men;
And Casey smiled—his rugged face no longer wore a frown,
The pitcher who had started all the trouble came to town.

All Mudville had assembled—yes, five thousand bugs had come,
To cheer the twirler who had put big Casey on the bum;
And when he stepped into the box the multitude went wild,
He doffed his cap in proud disdain—but Casey only smiled.

"Play Ball!" the umpire's voice rang out, and then the game began,
But in that peanut-eating throng no solitary fan
Could figure Mudville with a chance—and with the setting sun,
Their hopes sank low—the rival bunch was leading 4 to 1.

The last half of the ninth came round with no change in the score,
But when the first man up hit safe the crowd began to roar;
The din increased, the echo of five thousand throats was heard,
When the pitcher hit the second and then promptly passed the third.

Three men on base—nobody out—three runs to tie the game!
A triple meant the highest niche in Mudville's hall of fame;

But here the rally ended and the gloom was deep as night,
When the fourth one fouled to catcher and the fifth popped out to right.

A dismal groan in chorus came—a scowl was on each face,
As Casey walked out from the bench and started for his place;
His bloodshot eyes in fury gleamed, his teeth were clenched with hate,
He swung four bats with vicious swipes and then marched to the plate.

But fame is fleeting as the wind, and glory fades away,
There were no wild and woolly cheers—no glad acclaim this day;
They hissed and groaned and hooted as they hollered, "strike him out!"
But Casey gave no outward sign that he had heard this shout.

Here was his chance—and something snapped in Casey's tortured soul,
He felt his muscles bulge and strain, he felt the red blood roll;
He felt the crowd back on his head—he felt the touch of luck—
"Come on, you mug, and lay one through—but don't forget to duck."

The pitcher smiled and cut one loose—across the plate it sped,
Another hiss, another groan, "strike one!" the umpire said;
Zip—like a shot the second curve broke just above his knee,
"Strike two!" the umpire roared again—but Casey made no plea.

No roasting for the umpire now—his was an easy lot,
But here the pitcher whirled again—was that a rifle shot?
A whack! a crack! and out through space the leather pellet flew,
A speck against the distant sky—a blot against the blue.

Above the fence in center field in rapid whirling flight,
The speck sailed on—the blot grew dim, and then was lost to sight;
Five thousand voices called him king—five thousand threw a fit,
But no one ever found the ball that mighty Casey hit!

Each town must have its hero, though it turns at times to mock,
It doesn't matter who he is, so long as he can sock;
When I asked Casey how he felt—he looked up from his cup—
"That Thayer made a bum o' me—I had to show him up."[9]

The next ballad on the vindication of "Casey" occurred in a 1907 game,
long after his retirement. Bugville was playing some unknown opponent, and
"Casey" was a spectator in the stands. When the Bugville catcher was injured,
the call went out for a volunteer, and our hero offered his services. He proceeded to win the game and the pennant for Bugville. Oddly, no one recognized "Casey" until he identified himself.

THE VOLUNTEER

by C. P. McDonald—1908

The Bugville team was surely up against a rocky game,
The chances were they'd win defeat and not undying fame;
Three men were hurt and two were benched, the score stood six to four,
They had to make three hard-earned runs in just two innings more.

"It can't be done," the captain said, a pallor on his face,
"I've got two pitchers in the field, a mutt on second base";
And should another man get spiked or crippled in some way,
The team would sure be down and out, with eight men left to play.

"We're up against it anyhow as far as I can see,
My boys ain't hitting like they should and that's what worries me;
The luck is with the other side, no pennant will we win,
It's mighty tough, but we must take our medicine and grin."

The eighth round opened, one-two-three, the enemy went down,
The Bugville boys went out the same, the captain wore a frown;
The first half of the ninth came round, two men had been put out,
When Bugville's catcher broke a thumb and could not go the route.

A deathly silence settled o'er the crowd assembled there,
Defeat would be allotted them, they felt it in the air;
With only eight men in the field 'twould be a gruesome fray,
Small wonder that the captain cursed the day he learned to play.

"Lend me a man to finish with," he begged the other team,
"Lend you a man?" the foe replied, "my boy, you're in a dream;
We came to win the pennant, too—that's what we're doing here,
There's only one thing you can do—call for a volunteer."

The captain stood and pondered in a listless sort of way,
He never was a quitter and he would not be today!
"Is there within the grandstand here"—his voice rang loud and clear—
"A man who has the sporting blood to be a volunteer?"

And again that awful silence settled o'er the multitude,
Was there a man among them with such recklessness imbued?
The captain stood with cap in hand, while hopeless was his glance,
And then a short and stocky man cried out, "I'll take a chance."

Into the field he bounded with a step both firm and light,
"Give me the mask and mitt," he said, "let's finish up the fight.
The game is now beyond recall, I'll last at least a round,
Although I'm ancient you will find me muscular and sound."

His hair was sprinkled here and there with little streaks of gray,
Around his eyes and on his brow a bunch of wrinkles lay;
The captain smiled despairingly and slowly turned away,
When, "He's all right," one rooter yelled, another, "let him play."

"All right, go on," the captain sighed, the stranger turned around,
Took off his coat and collar, too, and threw them on the ground;
The humor of the situation seemed to hit them all,
And as he donned the mask and mitt, the umpire yelled, "Play Ball!"

Three balls the pitcher at him heaved, three balls of lightning speed,
The stranger caught them all with ease and did not seem to heed;
Each ball had been pronounced a strike, the side had been put out,
And as he sauntered to the bench, he heard the rooters shout.

One Bugville boy went out on strikes, and one was killed at first,
The captain saw them fail to hit and gnashed his teeth and cursed;
The third man smashed a double and the fourth man swatted clear,
Then, in a thunder of applause, up came the volunteer.

His feet were planted in the earth, he swung a warlike club,
The captain saw his awkward pose and softly whispered, "Dub!"
The pitcher looked at him and grinned, then heaved a mighty ball,
The echo of that fearful swat still lingers with us all

High, fast and far the spheroid flew, it sailed and sailed away,
It ne'er was found, so it's supposed it still floats on today;
Three runs came in, the pennant would be Bugville's for a year,
The fans and players gathered round to cheer the volunteer.

"What is your name?" the captain asked, "What is your name?" cried all,
As down his cheeks great tears of joy were seen to run and fall;
For one brief moment he was still, then murmured soft and low,
"I'm the Mighty Casey who struck out some twenty years ago." [10]

This verse provided the typical "comeback" format, wherein "Casey" banged a grand slam home run with two out and the count 0-and-2, in the last of the ninth inning to win the game.

CASEY—ACCORDING TO ANN A. NIAS

by Gordon Mackay—1912

Things were looking bleary for the Mudville nine that day,
The score was three to nothing, with an inning left to play;
The pitcher had a spitter that he broke around the knee,
And it looked as if on Mudville he would surely plant the bee.

The manager waxed sarcastic as his men went to the plate,
Took three swings at the floater and hit the backward gait;
That brought them to the players' bench, there to get a call,
While the pitcher sneered and put a lot of stuff upon the ball.

The ninth was on and Mudville still held its score at naught,
The game was getting fiercer and the lines were still held taut;
Not a hit had caromed through the game, and it looked to be all off,
While the air was filled with curses and the sounds of rooters' scoff.

Then Blake he swung and hit one that caused McMahon a boot,
And Sweeney pasted one that landed fair upon the snoot;
The pitcher lost his chipper smile, his face became as chalk,
While little Leary hit the paths with a ticket for a walk.

The crowd was crazed in rare delight as Casey lightly trod
To the blazon of the banner and the yelling of the god;
The umpire stuck his mask upon a face all set and grim,
While Casey never trembled with ten thousand eyes on him.

The pitcher swung his arm around a woobly little head,
He swung his arm, the ball sped true. "Strike one," the umpire said;
Casey glared in anger, as the most big leaguers do,
And murder lurked within his eyes as ump, he yelled, "Strike two."

Ten thousand eyes were fixed on him, five thousand tongues were still,
When, zowie, went old Casey's bat against the bobbing pill;
Oh somewhere in this favored land they tell that tale of yore:
How Casey met the pellet and he whanged it out for four.[11]

In this "comeback," "Casey" and Mudville faced the same old team and
the same old pitcher in the same old situation. Here, however, "Casey" came
off the bench and delivered a herculean homer that won the game.

CASEY THE COMEBACK

by Herman L. Schiek—1914

The Mudville fans were sick and sore for many a summer day,
And through the gloom in Mudville town there shone no cheering ray;
For the theme of every gossip, the talk in every hall,
Was how the mighty Casey had failed to hit the ball.

And Mudville scorned the mighty man who failed to win the fray,
They found their golden idol was made of common clay;
They called him every epithet their scorn could conjure up,
And everybody shunned him from the mayor to the pup.

That same old club came back one day that beat the Mudville nine,
That same old pitcher graced the slab and smiled a smile benign;
The Mudville fans looked on aghast, and 'twas with aching heart,
For Mudville veterans didn't have a look-in from the start.

The baseball battle fiercely raged beneath a scorching sun,
And in the last half of the ninth the score stood two to none;
Then Flynn again hit safely, to the wonderment of all,
And Blake again lambasted the leather from the ball.

Five thousand shouting fans went wild and beat the torrid air,
Pop bottles showered the ground like rain and gleamed like diamonds there;
They flashed the message to the town where whistles screamed like sin,
And e'en the church bells started loose and swelled the deafening din.

In the coacher's box the manager pranced wildly up and down,
He challenged nations to a fight, he blessed the good old town;
He yelled and whistled, pawed the air, and gave the tango dance,
And then he stood as petrified—for now was Casey's chance!

His eye shot toward the mourner's bench, where lonely Casey sat,
His cap pulled deep upon his face, his teeth sunk in his bat;
He saw the fire in Casey's eye—he saw his look of hate—
And then in accents hoarse and harsh he called him to the plate.

And from five thousand throats or more there rose a dismal groan,
The faces in the stands went white, the bleachers gave a moan;
A moan that had the sadness of the black and awful pit,
For Casey—he who lost that game—was asked to get a hit.

But Casey grimly grabbed his bat and at the plate he stood,
The pitcher smiled, the catcher laughed behind his wiry hood;
And Casey's face went red with wrath, and then grew deadly pale,
For once he knew how feels the dog with a tin can at his tail.

The first one over was too wide, but the umpire called it "fair,"
(He ought to have been flayed alive and roasted then and there);
The second one was far too low, but the umpire yelled "Strike tiew,"
And round the soul of Casey the air grew strangely blue.

A deathlike stillness gripped the fans, and e'en the groans had died,
There were no cheers for Casey now, but only, "Drat his hide!"
And again the pitcher loosed the ball, and again—but what was that?
It sounded like the crack of doom—but it came from Casey's bat!

Ten thousand eyes then saw the ball, as if it had been shot
From out some rifled cannon's mouth—and it traveled sizzling hot;

It swirled aloft o'er centerfield into the sky's clear blue—
It rapidly became a speck, then vanished from the view.

And then five thousand throats loosed up and yelled like men gone mad!
Ten thousand arms waved furiously, and hats went to the bad;
And from the blistering bleachers to the grandstand's swellest guy,
They wept and laughed and cussed and blessed till all their throats went dry.

Oh! Somewhere in our baseball land the shadows thickly fall,
The winds are sighing somewhere, and somewhere hangs death's pall;
And somewhere hearts are breaking, and towns are reft of fame,
But there is no gloom in Mudville, for Casey won the game.[12]

Nearing the age of seventy, "Casey" made an appearance in a game between Mudville and Midvale and belted a gargantuan homer in the last of the ninth on the first pitch.

CASEY'S COMEBACK

by Neil McConlogue—1922

It's been forty years or thereabouts since Casey gained renown,
Just because he couldn't clout the ball and knock it out of town;
The citizens of Mudville, who cheered that fateful day,
The young ones are all old folks and the old have passed away.

Still Mudville has her baseball team composed of faces new,
Of course there are no Cobbs or Ruths, it's a bush-league team, that's true;
So, I won't start criticizing the brand of ball they play,
I'm simply going to tell you what occurred the other day.

Now, I'm selling parts this summer for "the Hardly Able" car,
It's the fastest thing on rubber, from Maine to Ballston Spa;
When who should I meet, in Mudville, but my grand-sire, Hiram Bash,
With a pinchback suit of linen and a freshly-bobbed mustache.

He had complimentary tickets for the game that afternoon,
And when it comes to baseball, I'm a bleacher-shoutin' loon;
It seems the Mudville "Acorns" were to play the Midvale "Bears,"
And the game would be a hummer and was sure to raise the hairs.

Most every fan in Mudville, as well as some "fanettes,"
Had put their hard-earned money up to satisfy their bets;
That Midvale didn't have a chance with Mudville's hardy clan,
Oh! they backed the home team's chances, and they backed them to a man.

The innings came, the innings went, the seventh had gone by,
Five thousand throats in Mudville were tired, and very dry;
While on the field the athletes played errorless and true,
And when the ninth had rolled around the score stood two to two.

From the benches, black with people, there went up a lusty roar,
The Midvale bunch had had their bat—and failed to make a score;
Now a Mudville man makes second—No! "He's out," the umpire said,
While five thousand tongues in Mudville showered curses on his head.

Up from the home team's dugout, a stranger to each fan,
There came, in ancient uniform, a sadly battered man;
Whose hair had turned to silver; whose face was lined and seamed,
But upon whose florid countenance determination beamed.

The young fans didn't know him, the old ones there were few,
But when grand-pa saw his profile—"right in the air he flew;"
For this three-score-ten-year batter was the often talked about,
The sturdy, Mighty Casey who had, years before struck out.

And now the pitcher holds the ball, and now he lets it go,
Alas, the air is shattered by the force of Casey's blow;
And far off on the outskirts, some two miles from the game,
A baseball broke a window—also a window frame.

Oh! somewhere in this favored land the sun is shining bright,
The fans are cheering someone—and a player's heart is light;
For Mighty Casey's smiling, as he says he never knew
All the vigor he could garner from a goat gland that was new![13]

   In the following three poems, "Casey" is back in his prime, and he wins all
the games with grand slam home runs. The count and other details are not always mentioned, but the cruciality of the moment is apparent in all cases.

THE HERO

by Edgar Daniel Kramer—1925

All was still as death in Mudville when great Casey toed the plate,
With three runners on the hassocks, who would knot the grim debate;
He looked upon the pitcher with a stern and haughty stare,
Strike One! the umpire shouted, as the horsehide split the air.

Great Casey glared and grunted, then he took a firmer stance,
With his bludgeon on his shoulder and with hatred in his glance;
He swung with mighty fury and he smote the helpless blue,
As a slow ball cut the corner and the umpire called strike two!

Then the pitcher grinned at Casey, Casey spat disgust and frowned,
And the crowd just sat there breathless with no semblance of a sound;
Then they rose with frenzied shouting and with thunders of acclaim,
When great Casey met a fast one and his homer won the game.[14]

THE SAME OLD GAME

by L. H. Addington—1926

You've heard of Mighty Casey who dropped from baseball's fame,
Who swung and missed a third one, when he might have won a game;
From fandom's throne of idols Mighty Casey took a fall,
He was classed among the rummies when he swung and missed that ball.

All year he'd been the favorite of the patrons of the game,
For miles around the countryside they knew of Casey's fame;
But once he failed to hit the ball and all his glory flew,
They spoke of "Bonehead" Casey and told of how he blew.

He was ridden from the grandstand, the fans poured out their wrath,
Where once he walked on roses, there were brambles in his path;
But came a day not distant with a man on every sack,
Three runs'd tie and four would win, and Casey got his whack.

His wallop cleared the center fence, and as he rounded third,
He received a wild ovation, by action and by word;
Once more he's Mighty Casey, once more he's hailed as king,
Once more does fandom laud him, once more his praise they sing.

'Twas ever thus in baseball, you're a hero for a minute,
A bum when e'er you lose a game, a prince when e'er you win it.[15]

CASEY COMES BACK

by Oswald N. Burke—1929

The day that Casey fanned, he swore
He'd quit the game for evermore;
It grieved his heart and made him sore
To swing at empty air.
"I'm getting old. I've lost the range.
My back is weak. My knees feel strange.
I'll go to work—I need the change,"
Said Casey in despair.

"Aw can that stuff," Bill Jones replied,
"You'll knock that busher far and wide;
Next time he tries his low inside,

Keep cool and use your dome.
Just wait for one with lots of steam
Then swing and slap it on the seam;
You'll lose the ball and that's no dream,
They'll have to mail it home.''

But Casey vowed his arm was sore,
As from the bench he watched the score;
While Boston dropped a couple more
And slipped to second place.
And even when the vulgar herd
Began to pan him, not a word
From Casey's lips his teammates heard,
Nor sign crossed Casey's face.

Then Monday when the umpire cried
''Play Ball!'' the frenzied fans descried
That Jinx who'd lowered Casey's pride,
All warmed up for the game.
But Casey, mighty king of swat,
Was missing from the Boston lot;
His teammates searched but found him not,
While thousands toned his name.

The game went bad right from the start,
No wonder loyal fans lose heart
When swatters fail to do their part,
And swing likes gates ajar.
A deadly silence, like a pall,
Descended o'er the game of ball,
As thousands watched proud Boston fall,
Before a rising star.

The last half of the final round
Began, amid the shuffling sound
Of sullen rooters, homeward bound,
On tired and weary feet.
For with the count at one to four,
Why stick around and wait for more?
So, filing out, with spirits sore,
They headed for the street.

Bill Hicks, the first man up, struck out,
The game seemed lost, beyond a doubt;
When from the stands there rose a shout
That swelled to thunder tones.
And then was echoed, far and near,
A name, which pitchers never hear

Without a hint of something queer
A 'tingling in their bones.

'Twas Casey, held by law's delay,
While speeding onward to the fray!
With joyous shout the crowd gave way—
"Let's go! Put Casey in!"
But Casey only doffed his hat,
As on the bench he calmly sat,
While Jerry Dunn went forth to bat,
Amid a fearful din.

With raging fans on left and right,
The pitcher faltered, just a mite;
The ball, instead of breaking right,
Glanced off from Jerry's pate!
The noise increased into a roar
As Dunn took first—then led for more,
While Jones, who'd made a hit before,
Stepped briskly to the plate.

Jones drew a pass, and then the scene
Defied description. Jimmy Green,
Obeying orders, bunted clean,
And all three men were saved!
"Casey bats in place of Byrd!"
The umpire yelled, but no one heard;
Throughout the stands, from first to third,
Ten thousand maniacs raved.

As Casey headed for the plate,
With jaunty mien and easy gait,
Perchance the pitcher sensed his fate—
As eye met gleaming eye.
But if he felt his finish near,
He gave no sign and showed no fear,
But greeted Casey with a jeer
And let the first one fly.

The ball came up like lightning's flash,
To chance the first is sometimes rash,
But Casey met it with a crash,
Heard high above the din!
The ball went sailing through the air
And cleared the fence, with feet to spare;
Just where it landed, who should care?
With four runs racing in!¹⁶

Despite these heroic feats, the "Mighty Casey" did occasionally fail to "come back."

THE COMING BACK OF CASEY

by Charles E. Jestings—1937

A brilliant star was Casey out on Mudville's famous flat,
A ball-hawk in the field was he, a marvel at the bat;
His name was sought for autographs, his portrait for the wall—
Indeed, immortal Casey was the wizard of them all!

But even so, all Mudville tasted rank defeat that day,
When Casey, like a Brodie, let the pennant slip away—
A slim, ungainly hurler came advancing on the town,
And, working nicely in the pinch, set Mighty Casey down.

As Casey went out swinging, not a soul could shriek or shout,
The audience was petrified when Casey had struck out;
They couldn't feel, or hear or hope, but only see and sigh,
And fain believe this tragedy some black magician's lie.

Their thought to wreck the grandstand wasn't easy to resist—
There had so much depended on the ball Great Casey missed!
The thing stuck in the nimble mind of every rabid fan—
So everywhere that Casey went, they put him on the pan!

"A tennis racket, Casey!" "Strike out!" "Hit it with a board!"
The pack of wolves were on him now, a wild, abusive horde;
They rode him when he stepped to bat or gathered in a fly,
But Casey's only answer was the challenge in his eye.

One editor suggested to the club's aristocrats,
A trade involving Casey for a pair of real good bats;
And added, sort of slyly, that in case a deal went through,
There'd be no crime committed, nor could anybody sue!

From such humiliation would a timid novice fly,
'Twould cause bold veterans to cringe, or craven souls to die;
But calm, courageous Casey simply seemed to thrive on it,
And so the louder fandom razzed, the harder Casey hit.

As Casey's big bat echoed, one by one great records fell,
His specialty was homers, and the real old-timers tell
That when great Casey singled, he would streak to first and scowl,
As if to say, "That kind of hit's no better than a foul!"

Most frequently long homers did his brutal bludgeon pound,
As oft with devastated dreams, sad twirlers left the mound;
For Casey smashed them on the nose, he hit them low and high,
To settle down behind the wall or fade out in the sky.

Thus matters stood when Casey, in the spotlight of renown,
Faced once again the pitcher who before had set him down;
The Mudcats trailed by five to three in inning number nine,
With opposing factions deadlocked and the pennant on the line.

Yet Mudville's hopes most certainly were not forlorn at worst—
McCann had doubled, and when Cole beat out a bunt to first
With one away, the goose hung high and ready for the crate,
For Casey with his mighty bat was stepping to the plate!

There was art in every action, as he proudly took his stance,
That he meant to deal destruction was apparent at a glance;
And, when replying to applause, he waved up to the crowd,
The rousing roar that cheered him would have made a monarch proud.

But Casey didn't seem to hear; his keen and anxious eye
Glared at the gangling pitcher his most withering defy;
He dug his cleats into the turf like one who understands
Just how to settle briefly big business on his hands.

The hurler looked him over, coiled himself into a knot,
Then straightening, released the pellet forward like a shot!
Hard by the batter's waistline the fiery curve-ball shied,
"Too close for me!" said Casey. "Strike one!" the umpire cried.

The multitude, surprised, enraged, sent up a vicious groan,
Like a den of roaring lions bent on tearing flesh from bone—
The ump had called a rank one, but they couldn't rub him out—
They saw that far too many cops with billies stood about.

This robbery Great Casey did not protest or resist—
He took it smiling broadly like a big philanthropist;
With quiet ease of manner and with spirit unperplexed,
He stood as if announcing, "I am ready for the next!"

The gawky moundsman faced again his foeman from the hill,
No movement stirred the quiet air, the crowd grew very still;
And there in calm assurance and in patience all could feel,
Great Casey stood with waving bat and nerve as stout as steel.

The twirler gripped the ball; he paused; an instant held it high,
Then suddenly his arm came down and let it homeward fly!

There was a sharp, resounding smack that rang from wall to wall,
The sound a solid bludgeon makes when laid against a ball!

Throughout great cities there was joy and factory whistles blew,
And village bells rang lustily with a life of brighter hue;
And somewhere there was singing and 'most everywhere delight,
Because for someone, somewhere, almost everything went right!

And there was joy in Mudville, too! It was a jolly town!
It had its share of laughter, it basked in fine renown;
But *that* was, oh, *so* long ago! It was before that day,
When Casey, Mighty Casey, hit into a double play![17]

7.

"Casey" Carries On

Over the years writers placed "Casey" in a number of awkward and unique situations. In this collection of poems we find our hero, among other things, fraudulently claiming he played with "Cap" Anson on his famous Chicago team of the early 1880s, winning a game for Boston while in his cups, being banished from the club offices for refusing to sign a contract, exhibiting incredible honesty on a close play at home plate, pitching for Mudville with unexpected results on two occasions, playing cricket in England, and exploring outer space.

Grantland Rice, the most prolific composer of "Casey" poems, included this one in his collection of *Baseball Ballads* published in 1910. It is a parody of Eugene Field's "The Man Who Worked with Dana on the Noo York Sun."[1]

THE MAN WHO PLAYED WITH ANSON ON THE OLD CHICAGO TEAM

by Grantland Rice—1910

Thar showed up out in Mudville in the spring of '83,
A feller evidently just recoverin' from a spree;
He said his name was Casey, and he wuz a sight to view,
As he walked into the ball park, and inquired for work to do;
Thar wuzn't any openin', for you should understand
That wuz the time when Mudville had a bunch of stars on hand;
But the stranger lingered, tellin' Mickey Nolan and the rest,
What an all-fired battin' average he possessed when at his best;
Till finally he stated, quite by chance, as it would seem,
That he had played with Anson on the old Chicago team.

Wal, that was quite another thing; we owned that any cuss
Who's played with old Pop Anson must be good enough for us;
So we took Casey at his word and signed him while we could,
Well knowin' if we didn't that some other ball club would;
For Kankakee wuz lookin' round for people that could play,

And Pikeville wouldn't overlook this feller any day;
And we give him quite a contract, tho' it made the others swear,
Sayin' we had done 'em dirty and it wuzn't on the square;
But we laid back and cackled, for the pennant warn't no dream,
With the man who'd played with Anson on the old Chicago team.

It made our eyeballs nigh pop out and pop back in again,
To hear that Casey tellin' of old Anson and his men;
Why home runs wuz so common that nobody waved a hat,
With Williamson, King Kelly, or Fred Pfeffer at the bat;
A man who didn't hit above .500 couldn't stick
With that old bunch, for Anson would release him mighty quick;
They handled ground balls with their teeth and often shut their eyes,
While in the act of pullin' down the longest, hardest flies;
And after all the "fannin' bees" each night we used to dream,
Of the man who played with Anson on the old Chicago team.

But somehow this feller Casey never felt like goin' in,
He spent his time at Wilson's shakin' poker dice for gin;
Whenever he wuz needed he wuz always sure to shirk,
Remarkin' he would have to wait before he started work;
If any other gent had loafed the way he used to do,
We'd have fined him fifty dollars every day, and benched him too;
But you see the fans respected him and backed him to the last,
On account of his connections with the diamond in the past;
For no one felt like knockin' or handin' out a call,
To the man who'd played on Anson's team, the greatest of 'em all.

Wal, finally the climax came—the big test of the year—
And the fans wuz there in bunches from the country far and near;
Especially attracted by the statement made that day,
That, having rounded into shape, big Casey wuz to play;
The other nine was lookin' kinder worried and upset,
And they wouldn't even listen to an even money bet;
We kidded 'em and joshed 'em, but no wagerin' wuz done,
Till at last they placed a thousand at the odds of ten to one;
But even at these odds it looked an easy money scheme,
With the man who'd played with Anson on the old Chicago team.

But Casey never drew a chance to shine in any way,
They handed him a base on balls without the least delay;
The pitcher didn't seem to care to put one over straight,
While the man who'd played with Anson was a-standin' at the plate;
He only had one fly in left, which bounded off his head
(It seems the sun wuz shinin' in his countenance, he said);
And so the people waited in much anger and suspense
For Casey's opportunity to drive one through the fence;

And it came—O yes—it landed with a nauseating rap,
For the man who'd played with Anson, and referred to him as "Cap."

Old Mudville was a run behind when that last inning came,
The bases full and two wuz out—a hit would win the game;
"He's got to put it over now," each rooter waved his hat,
And shouted in delirium as Casey stepped to bat;
The first two inshoots jumped across the center of the plate,
As Mr. Anson's college chum found out a bit too late;
The next looked good and Casey swung—there came a mighty crack,
But the noise originated from the spine in Casey's back;
In reaching for that outshoot he had wrenched the spinal beam,
Of the man who played with Anson on the old Chicago team.

That night we wired Anson to discover if he knew
A man by name of Casey, as we felt we ought to do;
And when the answer came next day it stirred up quite a fuss,
"Yes, I remember Casey well—he carried bats for us."
We hunted for him quite a spell, but he had gone away,
Else the daisies would be bloomin' over his remains today;
But if you land in Mudville on the lookout for some fun,
Don't ever mention Casey's name unless you wear a gun.[2]

In the preceding chapter a portion of Grantland Rice's introduction to a poem dealing with "Casey's" "Yarvard" career was quoted because it contained Rice's statement that he authored "Casey's Revenge." The entire introduction is included here to supply background information on this disastrous adventure.

All remember [Rice wrote] how the mighty Casey lost the famed battle at Mudville by paddling the ozone in the last round of play. Later on we depicted the artful manner in which he secured his revenge, but it seems that after winning back his old fame he slumped again and was canned by Mudville. After losing out upon the diamond the ex-hero decided to try and recoup his lost fortunes on the gridiron. Old records show that he entered Yarvard college the next fall where early in the season his strength and speed made him a hero once more. And then came the final and deciding battle with Hale, where he drew another chance to win glory.

FAMED CASEY TURNS TO COLLEGE FOOTBALL

by Grantland Rice—1906

The outlook wasn't brilliant for the Yarvard bunch that day,
The score stood four to nothing, with two minutes left to play;
And when Hale's mighty halfback kicked a spiral thru the air,
A sickly silence fell upon all Yarvard's rooters there.

Most of them cursed and wailed aloud in deep despair, the rest
Clung to the hope which liveth on within each football breast;
They thought that if the captain would but let big Casey shine—
Well, the odds were good they'd cash in still if Casey hit the line.

But now the ball was eighty yards or more from Yarvard's goal—
That eighty yards looked farther than the distance to the Pole;
Not even mighty Casey, in all his strength and pride,
Could buck a rival line that hard, no matter how he tried.

But quicker than a lightning's flash their hopes began to mend,
When Smith, a sub, ran forty yards around Hale's strongest end;
And fond hopes bubbled forth anew when Jones, a freshman "shine,"
By lightning work, dashed down the field across the Ten-Yard Line!

Then from that bunch of Yarvard men there rose a mighty shout,
It echoed o'er the campus and re-echoed 'round about;
For when the dust had lifted there was no chance then to pine—
Two minutes left, and Casey poised to batter through the line!

The silence of eternity for one brief moment reigned,
And every eye was bulging out and every neck was craned;
The quarter's signal rang out clear and Casey made his dash,
AND THEN—Hale's forwards sifted through AND THEN—there came a smash.

They nailed big Casey by the feet and stood him on his neck,
They hurled him back ten yards or more and left him there, a wreck;
And some one grabbed the fumbled ball and dashed the other way,
While bleeding from a dozen wounds the mighty Casey lay.

Oh, somewhere in some college town, the students still may cheer,
And somewhere shouts of victory may ring out loud and clear;
But over Yarvard's campus now there hangs a heavy pall,
They buried Casey where he fell the day he dropped the ball.[3]

William F. Kirk wrote numerous baseball poems for the *New York Evening Journal*, which he later published in a little book called *Right Off the Bat*. The following ballad is one of several which have "Casey" playing with Boston.

CASEY ON A BAT

by William F. Kirk—1911

It looked extremely rocky for the Boston team that day,
The score was one to nothing, with one inning left to play;

Casey, who played in center field, had shown one hour too late,
He hadn't any alibi when staggering through the gate;
So when he tore his necktie off and stepped upon his hat,
The manager looked grim and said, "It's Casey on a bat."

"Well," said the Boston manager, "with joy I ought to scream,
Here's Casey with a dandy load, the best man on the team;
He told me he was sober, but he couldn't quite get by,
When he stepped upon his derby and was yanking off his tie;
Of all the hard luck in the world! The mean, ungrateful rat!
A blooming championship at stake and Casey on a bat."

Two Boston batters in the ninth were speedily retired,
"Here, Casey!" cried the manager, speaking as one inspired,
"Go in and bat for Grogan! There's a man on second base,
And if you hit the way you can we'll win the pennant race;"
This is no knock on buttermilk, or anything like that,
But the winning hit was made that day by Casey on a bat.[4]

The Federal League war provided choice materials for "Casey" parodists. The Federal League, an outlaw circuit unrecognized by Organized Baseball, began operations as a minor league in 1913. Little attention was paid to it until 1914 when it attempted to go big-time by raiding American and National League teams. The war raged throughout 1914 and 1915, but was finally settled following the 1915 season. A number of player jumps, salary wrangles, and court battles marked the conflict.

CASEY REDIVIVUS

Anonymous—1914

Oh, somewhere in this favored land the sun is shining bright,
And somewhere men can sleep in peace throughout the livelong night;
But baseball magnates tear their hair and toss on sleepless beds,
There is no peace in baseball—Mighty Casey's joined the Feds.[5]

This following verse was an outgrowth of several cases involving players who had jumped to the Feds. Hal Chase had just gone from the Chicago White Sox to the Buffalo Federals and the White Sox secured a temporary restraining order preventing him from playing with Buffalo. Bill Killefer, Phillies catcher, had also jumped—to the Chicago Federals—and then back again to the Phillies and the Chicago team sued to prevent him from playing with the Phillies.

CASEY AT THE PAY WINDOW

by George E. Phair—1914

When mighty Casey was enjoined the town was plunged in gloom,
The grandstand and the bleachers soon were lonely as a tomb;
The gate receipts are absent now, the magnate in despair
For no one cares to see a game if Casey isn't there.

But somewhere in this favored land, the lights are shining bright,
And Casey lingers there and gets a shine on every night;
For, though they shoo him from the field and will not let him play,
He doesn't care a whoop as long as Casey draws his pay.[6]

As the Federal League war heated up in the winter of 1914–1915, the Federal League went to court, demanding that the structure of Organized Baseball be dissolved as being a monopoly in violation of the antitrust statutes. The judge before whom the case was heard, Kenesaw Mountain Landis, later commissioner of baseball, held the matter under advisement for over a year, by which time the war was over. Landis was reluctant to render a decision during that time for fear that it might do serious damage to the national game. Grantland Rice caught the spirit and confusion of these legal shenanigans in this verse.

CASEY UP-TO-DATE

by Grantland Rice—1915

The outlook wasn't brilliant for a speedy court decree
As the judge's golf engagement was a quarter after three;
And so when Gilmore took his place, supplanting Garry's heft,
A sickly silence fell upon the few fans that were left.

A few poor boobs got up to go in deep despair, the rest
Clung to that hope which springs eternal in the baseball breast;
They thought if only Casey could but get a chance to land—
Well, they'd put up even money with old Casey on the stand.

But Ban preceded Casey with R. Ward amid the frame—
And one was quite a talker, and the other was the same;
So upon the stricken gathering woe laid a heavy hand
For there seemed but little chance of Casey's coming to the stand.

But Ban talked but an hour to the wonderment of all,
And Colonel Ward spoke even less before he left the hall;
Whereat the cheering echoes struck the court room with a jar,
For Casey, mighty Casey, was advancing to the bar.

There was kale in Casey's pockets as he stepped into his place,
There were contracts in his fingers—and a yawn on Casey's face;
And when, responding to the oath, he raised the proper hand,
Not a rooter in the place could doubt 'twas Casey on the stand.

The eyes of all were on him as he sought his counsel's ear,
The tongues of all applauded as he sent out for a beer;
And when the prosecutor put a hand upon each hip,
Defiance gleamed in Casey's eye—a sneer curled Casey's lip.

And now some pop-eyed lawyer started handing out hot air,
And Casey started lamping him in puzzled grandeur there;
Close by the sturdy batsman seven Latin phrases sped—
"Pro bono," started Casey, "I object," the lawyer said.

From the benches down below him there went up a muffled roar
Like growling that once echoed when he sought an umpire's gore;
"Kill him—kill that shyster!" shouted someone from the clan,
And it's likely they'd have mobbed him had not Casey winked at Ban.

With a smile of Blackstone wisdom mighty Casey's visage shone,
He called the court to order and he bade the judge go on;
He signalled to the lawyer who for several moments druled—
"I object," said Casey loudly—but the Judge yelled, "Over-ruled."

"Fraud," yelled the mad fanatics, and the echoes answered fraud,
But one legal look from Casey and the audience was awed;
They saw his face grow stern and cold—they saw his jawbone strain,
And they knew that Casey wouldn't boot that Latin phrase again.

They saw him call his counsel close and shake his burly fist,
They saw, and shuddered as they looked—a watch upon his wrist;
And when they handed him a bat, marked as Exhibit A—
He said, "That isn't in my line," and sadly turned away.

The sneer is gone from Casey's lip—his jaw began to crack,
A court attendant had to come and pound him on the back;
"Now tell us, old dog," said the Judge, "tell us who gets the dough,"
And Casey murmured, "Quod erat pro bono publico."

Oh, somewhere in this favored land they're playing games outdoors,
Somewhere the golfers bat the pill along the open moors;
And somewhere they have games today that still are partly sport,
But there is no joy in Balldom—Mighty Casey's gone to court.[7]

However the court suit turned out, "Casey" was not happy with his new contract. But everyone would agree that his demands—extreme for even those

Federal League days—would hardly have resulted in such treatment today. He no doubt would have turned to arbitration, or opted for free agency, or gone back to court.

IT'LL STAND ONE MORE PARODY

by Walter Trumbull—1915

There was ease in Casey's manner as he stepped into the place,
And a dime in Casey's pocket, and a smile on Casey's face;
While the other faces present bore expressions most benign,
For they needed Casey badly and they hoped he'd come to sign.

The owner of a ball club in the inkwell dipped a pen,
And shoved a contract over unto Casey there and then;
Close by the sturdy batsman the terms unheeded spread,
"That ain't enough," said Casey, "Whatell," the owner said.

Then from the throat of Casey came a loud and lusty roar,
"I ain't no busher, gents," he said, "so come across some more;
Ten thousand plunks a year, beside a signin' bonus sounds
About the thing. I'd also like a mortgage on your grounds."

'Twas somewhere on the outside land they noticed Casey light,
And he claims that birds were singing and stars were shining bright;
But the door was slammed so quickly that, though many were about,
No one could say exactly who threw mighty Casey out.[8]

Ten years after Grantland Rice described our hero's football failure at Yarvard, Harvard University produced an outstanding running back named Eddie Casey. He made Walter Camp's second team All-America in 1916, first team Service All-America in 1917, and first team All-America when he returned to Harvard in 1919. He also coached the "Crimson" from 1931 through 1934.[9] Thus Grantland Rice, writing for the *New York Tribune* in 1916, composed a poem about a real football star at Harvard named Casey. Unfortunately, only the first stanza of this verse was reprinted in the *Baseball Magazine*.

The outlook wasn't brilliant for the Harvard team that day,
The score was 10 to 0, with few minutes left to play;
If only Casey had a chance to ram the Tiger wall—
We'd put up even money now, if Casey had the ball.[10]

In introducing this verse, Gardner wrote: "In the many poems that have been written about Casey, little has been said of one of his most admirable character

traits: his unimpeachable honesty. The following ballad tells of a second unhappy occasion in which Mudville, thanks this time to Casey's inability to tell
a lie, also lost the game."[11]

CASEY AT THE PLATE

Anonymous—No Date

The Mudville hopes for victory were fading mighty fast,
The team was trailing nine to eight, the inning was the last;
And from the friendly bleacher bunch, there rose a vocal din,
"Don't worry, Boys! The game's the thing, and may the best team win!"

The Mudville catcher came to bat, they fanned him, one, two, three,
The second baseman popped a fly, the second out was he;
And then the crowd began to cheer—stupendous, hopeful, great,
For Casey, Honest Casey, was advancing to the plate!

The pitcher threw, and Casey swung, he hit the empty air,
Another pitch and Casey made his strikes an even pair;
And then a lusty bleacher voice, a helpful thought advanced,
"Go get the guy a snowshoe! Let him have a sportin' chance!"

The managers conferred and soon the fact was brought to light,
That each believed, "The customer is always in the right";
So Casey got a snowshoe and he slammed a hefty swat,
That sent the ball a sailin' to the corner of the lot!

The fielder ran to get the ball as Casey rounded first,
He picked it up as Casey got to second with a burst;
Of speed that took him on to third before the ball was tossed,
So Casey speeded down to home without a second lost.

Casey, ball and catcher came together at the plate,
And hope for Mudville dangled in the fickle hands of fate;
A hush descended on the fans who waited for the ump
To let them know if Casey was a hero or a chump.

All eyes were turned on Casey as the umpire scratched his head,
"I do believe in being frank and truthful, boys," he said;
"The play was close, I couldn't get a clear and ample view,
So to back a fair decision, I'll leave it up to you."

Oh, somewhere people brood about decadence of mankind,
They moan that truth and probity are mighty hard to find;
But Mudville hails an honest man whose heart is true and stout,
For Casey said, "I cannot lie. He tug me, boys, I'm out!"[12]

The first of "Casey's" two pitching appearances turned out to be a dream. His subconscious was in full command as he gained a special kind of revenge against his old adversary, Snedeker.

CASEY'S DREAM

by William F. Robertson—1936

As the dismal shades of evening gathered in his lonely room
All alone sat mighty Casey, staring at the murky gloom;
And the smile that once was Casey's now was covered with a frown,
For his crime had brought dishonor he could never quite live down.

So his head was bowed in sorrow, as he wondered just why Fate
Had so painfully restrained him as he stood there at the plate;
In his ears there still was ringing every tantalizing shout,
And he still could hear them telling how that pitcher struck him out.

As he sat there in the twilight wondering just what he'd do,
Asking if his shameful failure meant his baseball days were through;
Deep fatigue began to challenge and his strength began to creep,
Then his weary eyelids yielded, and poor Casey fell asleep.

Once again he heard the plaudits as he raced back to the wall,
And pulled down a mighty liner, to the wonderment of all;
And their words fell on his eardrums like a mother's lullaby,
And he told himself in secret he'd avenge himself or die.

Things looked bright for dear old Mudville, thanks to Casey's potent mace,
And that look of grim defiance crept again o'er Casey's face;
For he felt that his great comeback was another task well done,
And he knew he'd live forever in the hearts of everyone.

But the final inning started, as those last ones sometimes do,
And the pitching staff of Mudville seemed to suddenly fall through;
All were tried and all resembled water running from a ditch,
"Mr. Manager," said Casey, "let me go in there and pitch."

Arrogance again ruled Casey as he stepped into the box,
And again he was the captain of a ship upon the rocks;
But his heart leaped up with rapture as he proudly glanced about,
And discovered that the batter was the man who'd struck him out.

In the twinkling eyes of Casey confidence gleamed forth anew,
What a time and situation, what a spot to step into!
Two men out, the score all even, three men resting on the sacks,
And the promise from the pitcher that he'd stop 'em in their tracks.

Casey fell into his wind-up like a haughty, handsome prince,
And the ball went with a swiftness never seen before or since;
Momentarily they saw it, like the lightning in the night,
But they heard the sound of something stopping leather in its flight.

Just a foul, that's all, thought Casey, as again he looked around,
Then he stopped, and shrank with horror, for he saw there on the ground
Someone lying prone and helpless, resting on his earthly bed,
For the batter hadn't fouled it, but had stopped it with his head.

Oh the hand of fate cares little for the lowly or the great,
And the man on third had started and had dashed across the plate;
And the gallant sons of Mudville once again were put to rout,
And the cry went to the heavens, "Mighty Casey knocked him out!"

Then a gentle word of comfort fell again on Casey's ear,
"You have been asleep," said someone, "why you must be weary, dear;"
"Yes, I'm very tired," said Casey, "oh, this headache is a curse,
Could you give me something for it? I believe it's getting worse." [13]

"Casey's" second pitching performance might cause one to question the man's integrity, which was just established two poems ago.

CASEY ON THE MOUND

by Harry E. Jones—1954

It happened in the Bush League, not many years ago,
This little baseball incident, I think you ought to know;
Call it robbery or strategy, or by any other name,
It meant a lot to Crooksville, for Crooksville won the game.

'Twas a warm day in September, in the final play-off game,
The Crooksville boys were fighting, to gain the Hall of Fame;
For fifteen torrid innings they really gave their best,
The boys had played their hearts out, to win this final test.

Then came the sixteenth inning, when things began to hum,
On three successive singles Old Crooksville scored a run;
That little run looked mighty big, they eyed the board with pride,
They knew that all they had to do was to hold the other side.

The shades of night were falling when the boys took to the field,
To do or die for Crooksville, a score they must not yield;
The shades of night were falling as old Casey looked around,
The fans were filled with confidence, with Casey on the mound.

The first man up to face him went out on a fly,
Casey smiled with confidence at the cheer that rent the sky;
The next man went down swinging, two down and one to go,
The fans were begging Casey, "Make it three men in a row."

Then things began to happen, no one knows the reason why,
But it seems those pesky visitors had found their batting eye;
The next man up there singled, Casey kept him close to first,
But his pitching arm was aching, and old Casey feared the worst.

He was their only pitcher—they had used up all the rest,
In those fifteen torrid innings—so he vowed to do his best;
He threw his favorite sinker, but the fellow smacked the ball,
And the heart went out of Casey as he saw it hit the wall.

He was working very carefully now, and the cheering throng was stilled,
But Casey walked the next man, and the bases then were filled
With Slugger Bingo coming up, a trifle old but still
A regular bearcat in a pinch, this boy could swat the pill.

With Casey really bearing down, the count was three and two,
A hit now meant the ball game, how well old Casey knew;
He looked out at his fielders, he gazed up at the sky,
He had a grin upon his lips, and the devil in his eye.

He signaled to the catcher and strolled toward the plate,
They met there on the pathway, strategic plans to make;
"It's getting dark," said Casey, "and difficult to see,
If we're to win this ball game, I think it's up to me."

"So I'll go through the motions of throwing you the ball,
Yes, I'll go through the motions, but without a ball at all;
You act as though you make the catch, I'll wait 'til you're all set,
It's going to take this strategy to win this ball game yet."

Then Casey walked back to the mound, and dusted off his hand,
Then peered in at the catcher with a manner that was grand;
He took his finest wind up, though he felt so queer inside,
Then whipped his arm and let 'er go, "Strike three!" the umpire cried.

Old Slugger Bingo, white with rage, pounded on the plate,
The things that he was saying are too sad to relate;
But when he'd cooled enough to speak, he grabbed the ump and cried,
"You blind old bat, you know that ball was a good two feet outside!" [14]

"Mighty Casey" never lost his love for baseball, and when his playing days were over he became a dedicated fan. One is puzzled, however, as to why he would only root for the Giants.

CASEY AS A FAN

by Russell Askue—1924

Oh, where is mighty Casey, whom the fans did once adore?
Oh, where is mighty Casey, since his playing days are o'er?
He's pulling for the Giants now, as only Casey can,
For grim and grizzled Casey, is a lusty, roaring fan.

He tells the shortstop how to stop, the pitcher how to throw,
The catcher when to block a steal, the runner when to go;
Heroic Casey was a tower of strength when in his prime,
But watch him now—he does the work of nine men at a time.

When plays are breaking badly, and the battle is in doubt,
Old Casey bids the boys hang on, and fight each inning out;
But when a batting rally's on, 'tis grand above the din,
To hear his joyous bellow urging all the runners in.

Now Casey is a fighter, as all loyal fans agree,
And no one pulls for victory more desperately than he;
But from his playing days one memory comes to make him flinch—
Proud Casey bows in silence at a strike-out in a pinch![15]

Reports of "Casey's" drinking are mixed, you might say, but there is clear evidence that he had a weakness for the gaming rooms. However, his luck there was no better than on that momentous day in Mudville.

CASEY AT THE DICE

by Frank Jacobs—1969

The table wasn't breaking for the Vegas crowd that night,
The house was up 12 thousand with no change of luck in sight;
So, when Epstein came out snake-eyes, and Spinelli missed his point,
A mood of deep depression could be felt throughout the joint.

The dollar-bettors, cleaned of cash, were heading out the door,
But all the big high-rollers stayed to even up the score;
They said: "If only Casey had a chance to roll the dice,
We'd have a shot to change our luck, which now is cold as ice."

Then, suddenly, their eyes lit up, a cry rose from their lips,
It echoed off the slot machines, it rattled off the chips;
It rumbled through the Black Jack games while cards were being dealt,
For Casey, lucky Casey, was advancing to the felt!

His nails were cleanly manicured, his face was richly tanned,
His suit was iridescent silk that cost him half a grand;
The cuff-links on his sheer batiste were rubies from afar,
Between his teeth he coolly smoked a ninety-cent cigar!

There was ease in Casey's manner as he calmly placed his bet,
His hands were steady as a rock, his palms were free of sweat;
The other shooters, now revived, together had one goal,
To place each C-note they had left on Casey and his roll!

With confidence and quiet pride he gripped the cubes of white,
Then, blowing on them softly, he prepared them for their flight;
"A seven, dice," he murmured, as he looked up to the sky,
And a hush went 'round the table as he raised his arm on high!

The cool is drained from Casey's face, his eyes are tense and keen,
And all along his sun-drenched brow deep furrows can be seen;
And now he firmly holds the dice, and now he lets them go,
And now the air is shattered by the force of Casey's throw!

Oh, somewhere in this wealthy land there is a happy spot,
Where naturals are being rolled and dice are running hot;
And somewhere men are doubling up and winners scream and shout,
But there is no joy in Vegas—Lucky Casey has crapped out![16]

The next two poems in this chapter were written by an Englishman, J. A. Lindon. They were published for the first time in Gardner's *Annotated Casey*.

A VILLAGE CRICKET CASEY

by J. A. Lindon—1967

It had been a sticky wicket at Cowpat-under-Slosh,
A day of storm and sunshine, of heat and mackintosh;
And now, 6 down for 39, they feared that they must lose,
To the visiting eleven from Mudlark-in-the-Ooze.

They needed only 50, but their play was out-of-joint,
For Joe Darke, who was Sexton, spooned a dolly-catch to point;
And little "Bunny" Scutters was bowled around his legs,
By a ball that pitched a yard wide—then broke, and took his pegs.

Thin Skinne came in with Blockham, there were jabs and Chinese cuts,
(Tail-enders both—good bowlers, but they couldn't bat for nuts);
So hopes were pinned on Casey, "Hard" Casey from the forge,
An iron-muscled blacksmith, he could *hit* the ball, by George!

Skinne hooked a lucky single, then Blockham flicked a four,
Which meant that six were needed to make the winning score;
Schoolmaster hollered, Shepherd bleated, Parson waved his beer,
And Wally Thatcher, up a tree, fell plop! into the weir.

Then Blockham thought he'd "have a go"—the Umpire came to put
The bails back on his shattered stumps—he'd missed it by a foot!
And the shocked and awful silence that greeted his decease,
Became a yell, for Casey was advancing to the crease.

Grim-smiling and determined, he came striding up the pitch,
Like a mighty Alex Bedser (maybe Eric, who knows which?);
He sported no white flannels, he scorned to wear a cap,
But in dungarees, bare-chested, he stood to fill the gap.

A hundred eyes were on him, even goats there on the green
Stopped grazing for a moment, said "Maaahh!" when they had seen
The Umpire give him center, which he marked with heavy thumps,
Then, standing up, he scrutinized the field about his stumps.

Behind him crouched the keeper, as bald as any egg,
(The Mudlark village grocer), slip, gully, backward leg;
Before him only cover, the rest were on the ropes,
Awaiting lofty mis-hits from this man of Cowpat's hopes.

Now he is hunched and ready, the bowler with a cough,
Slings down a ball that curves away, then nips in from the off;
And Casey whirls a mighty bat which doesn't quite connect,
And everybody gulps to see his wicket still erect.

The bowler licks his finger, flips back his hair, and comes
Jig-hopping up to bowl again; the spinning leather hums
And dips and bounces on the pitch where ducks can be a scandal,
And Casey swipes at it so hard his blade flies off the handle!

Good Parson now is praying, Schoolmaster dare not look,
Old Shepherd unawares has tied a sheepshank in his crook;
All know if Casey should connect he'll score the winning clout,
But if he misses once again most likely he'll be out.

Another bat is brought him, his blade taps in the block,
A golden note comes belling from the old church-tower clock;

The bowler whips the leather down, all wait for victory,
And even Wally Thatcher has found another tree.

Oh what a SHOUT OF TRIUMPH as the wicket fails to fall!
Oh what a SHOUT OF TRIUMPH at the sound of bat and ball!
Oh what a SHOUT—from Mudlark—as Casey, moved by care,
Prods with excessive caution, and pops it in the air![17]

With the launching of the space program in the 1950s and with the first manned
space flight in the 1960s, it was only to be expected that someone would con-
vert "Casey" into an astronaut. It was the aforesaid Englishman, Lindon.

CASEY IN THE CAP

by J. A. Lindon—1967

Moon looked a rocky target to America that day,
Of late too many cosmonauts up there had lost their way;
And after James Scott Gussilpard had vanished without trace,
Taking Walter Edward Staffitt, there was tension at the base.

"It's a game of snakes-and-ladders, life and prestige are the stakes,
And you must keep mounting ladders, not come sliding down the snakes";
Mused Dr. William Lee, "Go wrong? With any other chap,
But we shall soon be on the Moon with Casey in the cap!"

The mighty Saturn booster had sent roaring into space,
The fifth Apollo capsule of the get-'em-up-there race;
And now, with lunar bug attached and ready soon to land,
In orbit round the Moon it lay with Casey in command.

First, Colonel Grisson Glenn McWhite had through the tunnel crawled,
Then Schirra Young B. Carpenford had followed unappalled;
A button sealed the hatches and the Lem fell like a glove,
To spiral swiftly moonward, leaving Casey up above.

He shot the message back to Base, "Decoupling gone O.K.,"
Cape Kennedy relayed it far beyond the USA;
On tellies by the million it went flashing round the earth,
Or cracking out of radios from Pontypool to Perth.

Oh what a shout of human pride went up next from the world!
What tears of joy and kissing! Oh the homburgs that were hurled;
Aloft to meet the ticker-tape when, shortly after noon,
The message came from Casey, "They have landed on the Moon!"

A hundred million misty eyes were focused on the sky,
Or held in thrall by telly, fifty million throats were dry;

As countdown for the blast off of the lunar bug drew near,
To "4–3–2–1-Zero!" then "Ignition!" then "They're clear!"

And Schirra Young B. Carpenford and Grisson Glenn McWhite,
Up from the lunar surface rose in pioneering flight;
To where Commander Casey, very watchful now and stern,
In orbit round the Moon would be awaiting their return.

The Lem pursued Apollo, but the link-up didn't come,
For something must have happened—Casey's radio was dumb;
The telly went on working, all could see (though it was blurred)
That Casey *looked* attentive—but he didn't say a word!

Then over Casey's features came a sudden happy smile,
Which lulled the consternation of those watching—for awhile;
As gadgets all about him flickered "Link up!" from the Lem,
And Casey *looked* attentive—but he wasn't heeding *them*.

"God rot the guy!" exploded Lee; Cape Kennedy went mad,
A hundred million eyes on earth could see that things were bad;
As Schirra Young B. Carpenford and Grissom Glenn McWhite,
Tried for their third and final link, then vanished—into night.

The smile is gone from Casey's lip, his eyes are bulging out,
His tongue goes licking to and fro, he would not hear a shout;
Excitedly he turns a page, ejaculates "Gee whizz!"
He is reading Science Fiction, he's forgotten where he is!

Oh somewhere two poor cosmonauts are flying through the void,
Both feeling most uneasy lest they meet an asteroid;
And somewhere they may light on one, and perish with a slap,
But never they'll link up again with Casey in the cap.[18]

Following the publication of *The Annotated Casey at the Bat*, Martin Gardner received a letter from a reader who recalled a 1915 or 1916 verse which sent our hero to the Great Beyond. However, the reader could only remember the first line and the final stanza. It began with "Now Casey's gone to Kingdom come, where all good players go. . . . " He at length reached the pearly gates.

"The outlook wasn't brilliant"—that's as far as Casey got,
When Peter grabbed him by the pants, and down the chute he shot;
Then turning to St. Gabriel, he dusted off his hat,
Remarking, "That's the last we'll hear of Casey and his bat."[19]

St. Peter proved to be in error, however, as the following poem attests.

MIGHTY CASEY'S GHOST

by Sylvester R. Miller—1909

So they buried poor old Casey in the cemetery plot,
And chiseled on his headstone, "Here lies a Son of Swat
Who failed to 'line 'er out' in that game the other day,
And we've given him good burial where we hope that he will stay."

But on the stilly summer eves the natives often say
That Casey's ghost comes from his grave and beats it for the fray;
He still imagines he's at bat; the multitude is hushed,
The same old smile is on his face, his brow with triumph flushed.

The umpire yells "Strike two!" again and Casey hears the cry
Of ghostly voices in the stands to "bang it to the sky";
And once again the pitcher heaves the pellet without fear,
And once again poor Casey fans the torrid atmosphere.

With mournful tread he wends his way back to his silent grave,
Where through the lonesome hours of night the people hear him rave
Of days when he was Mudville's Pride; of games he'd ended quick
With one grand, soul-inspiring clout from his immortal stick.

So take heed all ye slammers with marks .300 strong,
Play the game each minute and take what comes along;
Smash the first good hot one that sails across the pan,
Don't wait the way poor Casey did, for he's an "also-ran."[20]

8.

The Family

In the "Casey" literature, the wife, sister, daughter, and three sons of the slugger have attained immortality. In this group of six family poems, as might be expected, numerous inconsistencies and improbabilities arise.

MRS. CASEY AT THE BAT

Anonymous—No Date

'Twas the day of the great big softball game with the Boltsy Nutsy Frails,
The score stood eighteen-twenty and six broken fingernails;
And when Betty turned her ankle and Ethel burst a seam,
The fans were so disgusted they were almost fit to scream.

A straggling few got up to go and get a malted milk,
The rest swapped recipes or showed each other bits of silk;
For they felt the girls had let them down particularly flat,
Unless—and quite unlikely—Nellie Casey got to bat.

Dot Flynn preceded Nellie, to say nothing of Mae Breen,
And the less you said the better, if you know just what I mean;
Though don't ever say I said it—they were both of them too fat,
There was little chance of Mrs. Casey getting to the bat.

But Flynnsie shut her eyes and swung (it almost killed them all),
And Maisie did a rhumba which connected with the ball;
And when the dust had lifted—well I'll be a dirty word,
There was Maisie Breen on second, and Dot Flynn was safe on third.

Then the stands reverberated with soprano shrieks of glee,
Their wads of gum they swallowed when the fans thought what they'd see;
And two girls kissed each other (though each thought each a cat),
For Mrs. Nellie Casey was advancing to the bat.

How they clapped for Mrs. Casey as she stepped into her place,
Her corset fitted perfectly, she moved about with grace;
This was her chosen universe of which she was the hub,
(While back in their apartment, Casey waited for his grub).

"Well, throw the ball, Estelle," she cried, "and get it over, do!"
And blushing with self-consciousness, the Boltsy pitcher threw;
"By me," said Mrs. Casey, in her best bridge-player's voice,
"It's much too low!" But just the same, "Strike!" was the umpire's choice.

"You nasty man!" the girls went wild, in accents loud and shrill,
"You brute! You boor! You peasant! You idiot! You pill!"
"Oh, kill him! Kill him!" were the cries that rose from out the stand,
They'd have beaned him with their compacts had not Nell held up her hand.

With savoir-faire that would have drawn a nod from Mrs. Post,
She signaled for the second pitch and stilled the angry host;
"Come on, Estelle, try hard, dear, do—you know the kind I like,"
Again the ball came over and again the ump cried "Strike!"

"Boo!" screamed the crowd. The catcher grinned, "It's raw, but don't you mind,
The shine from off your nose, my dear, has drove the umpire blind;"
That's all that Mrs. Casey heard. That's all, but 'twas enough,
A shiny nose—five thousand fans—and where's her powder puff?

The Casey smile is set and grim; no longer does she speak,
Her thoughts are in the Powder Room, and on that gleaming beak;
And now the pitcher holds the ball, and now she lets it go,
And now the air is shattered with Mrs. Casey's blow.

Oh, somewhere in this favored land, good husbands get a break,
Somewhere they feast on crisp french fries, and tender, juicy steak;
But a girl can't bat with a shiny nose, of that there is no doubt,
So Casey eats cold beans tonight, Mrs. Casey has struck out.[1]

"Casey's" younger sister, Hortense, also duplicated her brother's act in this game against Vassar. Since the poem's author did not precisely set forth the family connection between brother and sis, Gardner happily clarified the relationship in an introductory note.

CASEY THE SECOND

by James O'Dea—1911

What! You missed the big game, and you'd have me tell
Your friend of the manner in which we fell

To the Vassar eight with our speed reversed?
I will—if you introduce me first.

Charmed! I assure you—Why, surely, indeed,
We play only eight on a side—Agreed;
For the sun-field can freckle till one is incensed,
So, with that position we girls have dispensed.

Well, the Vassar Delights—all lovely girls, too
Came up from their varsity bringing a crew
Of rooters and fans whose desire, it would seem,
Was to jump on the necks of our lady-like team.

And all through the game they were dreadfully rude,
My dear, it was shameful as fiercely they boo'ed;
And shouted, "Oh, sweet!" and "Why don't you slide!"
With a lot more unheeded advice on the side.

The game as a contest was perfectly cute,
Except for the umpire, and he was a brute;
From the talk that went 'round I should judge the old dunce,
Was a robber, a blockhead and fool all at once.

For eight hands around—Yes, innings, I mean,
'Twas the darlingest thing of the kind I have seen;
Twenty-three—twenty-three was the score on the fence,
Precisely—a tie—with excitement intense.

When the Vassars got through with their stunt at the bat
In the ninth and last innings I thought it was "scat!"
For the girls of our side, for when finished, they had
Five runs to the good which, of course, made it bad.

But we didn't care though the going seemed rough,
Not one of our crowd even wilted a puff;
Till two of our team were put out—so were we,
Wanting two extra runs if the winners we'd be.

"But wait!" said a girl at my side who was "wise,"
"Just wait till we hand 'em the gentle surprise;
Are we there with a something concealed up our sleeve?
Just rub up your glasses and see, and believe!"

"Ah! here she is now! Can you beat her for class!
Will she get the runs? Will a rabbit eat grass?
'Who is she?' Why, Casey, Hortense Casey who
Can lace that old ball as she'd lace her own shoe."

With two on the bases and fire in her eyes,
To the plate she advances and somebody cries:
"Now, Casey, come on, put it over the fence,"
"You bet you, I will," said the smiling Hortense.

And then it began—Well, I'd rather not say,
What was said to the umpire that memorable day;
As there he stood calling, "Strike One!" and "Strike Two!"
All umpires are horrid, I think so, don't you?

"And now," said the girl who was wise, "this is It—
That pitcher is there with a pretty good 'spit,'
But watch dear old Casey cut loose with a swat
That will land it beyond the confines of the lot."

The ball comes to Casey, who swings with her bat,
And fiercely she strikes—where the ball isn't at—
The catcher has caught it—complete is the rout,
With "His Umps" saying: "Sister, that's three and you're out!"

And that's how we happened to lose the big game,
There was nothing momentous about it, I claim;
Except for the tale that it turnishes—that
Of Casey the Second who failed at the bat.[2]

Although Gardner spoke of only one son of the "Mighty Casey," Angus,
two other ballads dealing with the slugger's male offspring have been published. It is conceivable that the three poems refer to the same young man, but
their content seems to argue against such a supposition.

THE LEAGUE OF LONG AGO

by William F. Kirk—1911

They've got me sitting on the bench—I knew it had to come,
Kid Casey subbed for me at third the day I broke my thumb;
My thumb got better fast enough, but when I wanted back,
"The Kid is stinging them a mile," says good old Captain Mack.

"The Kid is running bases like a Murray or a Cobb,
The Kid does this, the Kid does that, the Kid is on the job;"
And so I'm sitting on the bench, my spirits sort o' low,
And playing memory ball games in the League of Long Ago.

I'm pulling for Kid Casey, and I hope he makes a mint,
I help him every way I can, from cussword down to hint;

He knows that I am for him, too—'twas only yesterday,
He says to me, "Old leaguer, you've got ten more years to play."

But I know that he knows better, and I know just what I'm worth,
A man can't last forever in the swiftest game on earth;
And so I'm sitting on the bench, my spirits sort o' low,
And playing memory ball games in the League of Long Ago.

I played with Old Buck Ewing just before Buck blew the game,
I played with Jimmy Ryan in the days of Anson's fame;
Then I was just a fresh young kid, and they were getting old,
But not one slur they gave me when I broke into the fold.

That's why I like Kid Casey, and I'll plug like sin for him,
I told Mack only yesterday my eyes were getting dim;
And so I'm sitting on the bench, my spirits sort o' low,
And playing memory ball games in the League of Long Ago.[3]

CASEY'S SON

by Ferguson Fague—1911

August
The baseball fans of Mudville had spent a sleepless night,
For the "Son of Mighty Casey" had fanned with all his might;
Three healthy swings he had, and then, his one-time glory faded,
The rooters jeered and roasted him as homeward they paraded.

September
The Mudville baseball season was drawing to a close,
The two teams that were leading had been fighting nose to nose;
First one and then the other would hold the lead a day,
Until the other came along and took it right away.
Ninety games had each team played, seventy each had won,
The championship, would settled be before another sun;
Each line-up had their strongest men, all eager for the fray,
And everyone was ready when the Umpires yelled out "Play."

Skilman, for the Mudville boys, had curves and speed galore,
His "spitball" too was breaking, as it never had before;
The Slamtown's blonde-haired twirler, "Reddy" Swift by name
Was "warming up" in practice, in keeping with his fame.
The game was fast and scoreless, and eight innings had gone by,
When Mudville's kid third baseman let drop an easy fly;
A stolen base, a sacrifice, advanced the man to third,
"A hit! A hit! of any kind," was all that could be heard.

Two balls were called and then a strike, upon the waiting batter,
The "Umpire's" voice could scarce be heard, drowned by the din and clatter;
The next ball pitched the batter struck, lined out a pretty single,
The Slamtown team, now wild with glee, had scored upon that bingle.
The next man was an easy out, from third to first retired,
A fly, then Slamtown took the field, with confidence inspired.
The Mudville nine were now at bat, their last time it is true,
But "Courage" still was with them, and would stay the whole game through.

The first man fanned, then "Sure-Eye" Smith, was passed to first on balls,
"Scaggs" was told to "hit 'er out," by many rooters' calls;
Instead he laid a little bunt, right down the first base line,
Which pitcher nor first sacker could handle quite in time.
Both runners were advanced a base, upon an infield out,
A hit was what was needed to make all Mudville shout;
Up at the plate Young Casey stood, with bat at graceful poise,
Waiting for the ball he liked, amid an awful noise.

The pitcher sent an in-shoot, a-speeding cross the plate,
The batter made a vicious swing, but just a second late;
Three balls were called and then a strike, and everybody knew,
That if the next ball was not hit the game would then be through.
The next one was a daisy, and "Casey" met it fair,
Both runners had just crossed the plate before the ball got there;
Onto the field the frenzied fans rushed forth to meet their crack,
But "Casey" pushed them all away and wildly waved them back.

" 'Twas just a month or so ago," he said, "you jeered and shouted
'That lobster cannot hit a ball. He's not what he's been touted,'
But now I've made a luck hit, that scored a needed run,
You're all too anxious now to be a friend of Casey's son."
The baseball fans of Mudville, will tell you of that game,
Who won it, how and what he did, that "Casey" was his name;
Forgotten is the day he whiffed, the day his friends deserted,
To "Casey," glory, fame and friends have rightfully reverted.[4]

Angus had the desire and ambition to play the game, but his odd construction doomed him to disappointment, at least as far as a professional career was concerned. But he did play some sandlot ball for Mudville when in his teens, and he did hit the long ball much like his father. An amusing incident involving Angus in a game with the Slamtown sandlotters in 1905 was narrated by Nitram Rendrag.

CASEY'S SON

by Nitram Rendrag—1967

The game had almost ended, the sun was hanging low,
Slamtown was leading six to three, one inning yet to go;
Two outs for Mudville, none on base, with Dibble at the plate,
And Dibble's batting average was the lowest in the state.

But Dibble drove a double, much to everyone's surprise,
And when Pringle binged a bingle, you should have heard the cries!
With Dibs on third and Pring on first, the hopes of Mudville rose,
For the son of Mighty Casey was advancing on his toes.

Yes, the son of Mighty Casey tiptoed carefully to his place,
There was caution in his bearing and a frown upon his face;
In the dugout he'd been guzzling beer and never dreaming that
He'd have the opportunity of getting up to bat.

Young Casey was a trifle plump, but had a lot of guts,
The fans all called him "Butterball" or sometimes just plain "Butts";
His height: five feet, five inches, his weight: two hundred pounds,
His habit: whacking balls beyond the borders of the grounds.

Young Casey burped and swung and missed, a rooter bellowed "Boo!"
He swung and missed and burped again, the ump called out "Strike Two!"
The third was high, the fourth was low, the fifth pitch grazed his cheek,
Casey hitched his beltless pants, he gave his cap a tweak.

The pitcher winds, he cuts it loose, young Casey shuts his eyes,
He swings a monstrous swing and—crack!—the pill is in the skies;
Dibble dances home while Pring is prancing on to third,
And Casey's rounding first, the ball's still winging like a bird.

The men in left and center fields are racing toward the sphere,
When Pringle trots across home plate, the fans jump up and cheer;
"I've got it!" shouts one fielder, the other yells "She's mine!"
They bump, they fall, the baseball smacks an advertising sign.

It bounces back, one man gets up, retrieves it, throws it, stumbling,
While Casey gallops on to home, perspiring, stomach rumbling;
A mighty burp! two buttons pop, his legs are tied in knots,
His trousers hang below his knees, his shorts have polka dots!

Poor Casey's face is cherry red, he trips and almost falls,
He tries to pull his trousers up, alas, too late, the ball's
Now nestled in the catcher's mitt, young Casey spins and snorts;
He heads for third but feels the pill that's pressed against his shorts.

Somewhere tonight, in Kansas, there are happy men and boys,
Who are celebrating victory and making lots of noise;
There is singing, dancing, laughing, but it's in another town,
There is only gloom in Mudville since poor Casey's pants fell down.[5]

Thirteen years after Mrs. Casey struck out in a softball game—that was in 1906—Casey's daughter Patsy had an opportunity to redeem the honor of the distaff side of the family. However, in this match between Centerville and Mudville that was not to be.

CASEY'S DAUGHTER AT THE BAT

by Al Graham—1939

The outlook wasn't brilliant for the Mudvillettes, it seems,
The score stood four to two against the best of softball teams;
And when Brenda "Lefty" Cooney and "Babs" Barrows both flied out,
A sickly silence filled the air, and the fans began to pout.

A straggling few got up to go—'twas the ninth and two were down,
While the rest had little hope at all that the 'Ettes would go to town;
Still, they thought if only Casey's gal—Patricia—Patsy—Pat,
Could get a lick, they still might win with Casey at the bat.

But Myrna Flynn and Hedy Blake had to hit before Miss C.,
And the former was a sissy, and the latter just a she;
So again upon a Mudville throng grim melancholy sat,
For there seemed no chance whatever that Patricia'd get to bat.

But Myrna smacked a single, to the wonderment of all,
And Hedy—known as Flatfoot—fairly flattened out the ball;
And when the dust had lifted, there on third and second base,
Perched a pair of Mudville cuties, each a-powdering her face.

Then from the howling mamas in the stand in back of first,
Went up a weird, unearthly scream, like a Tarzan crazed with thirst;
Like a million screeching monkey-fans, like a yowling giant cat,
For Casey, Patsy Casey, was advancing to the bat!

There was ease in Patsy's manner as she stepped up to the plate,
There were curves in Patsy's figure, and a bounce in Patsy's gait;
And when responding to the screams she lightly doffed her hat,
No Casey fan could doubt 'twas Mighty's daughter at the bat.

Ten thousand eyes were on her shorts, an orchidaceous hue,
Five thousand tongues commented on her blouse of beige-and-blue;

And while the ladies chattered ''What a shape!'' and ''What a fit!''
Miss Casey gave her shorts a tug and smoothed her blouse a bit.

And now the underhanded pitch came hurtling through the air,
But Patsy, like her famous dad, just stood a-smiling there;
And when ''Strike One!'' the umpire yelled as past that softball sped,
''That ain't my style!'' is what they say Patricia Casey said.

Again, as in the years a-gone, the crowd set up a roar,
Again, they shouted as they had so many years before;
''Kill him! kill the umpire!'' and as once did Patsy's Pop,
Miss Casey raised a staying hand, and mildly said, ''Oh, stop!''

And smiling like a lady in a teethy toothpaste ad,
Patricia showed that howling mob she wasn't even mad;
She signaled to the pitcher, who again the ball let fly,
And again like Papa Casey's, Patsy's second strike went by.

Anew, the maddened thousands blamed the strike upon the ump,
A racketeer, they labeled him, a floogie, and a frump;
But once again the mob was stilled by Patsy's charming smile,
As certain every fan became she'd hit the next a mile.

And now they see her daub a bit of powder on her nose,
They watch her put fresh lipstick on—a shade called Fleur de Rose;
And now the pitcher holds the ball, and now she lets it go,
And now the air is shattered by *another* Casey's blow.

Oh! somewhere in this favored land the moon is shining bright,
And somewhere there are softball honeys winning games tonight;
And somewhere there are softball fans who scream and yell and shout,
But there's still no joy in Mudville, Casey's *daughter* has struck out.[6]

9.

Parodies

By far the largest group of "Casey" poems were parodies, either of "Casey" himself, or of the dramatic situation when he came to bat. Many of these verses were takeoffs on important recent events in the baseball world, or occasionally, in the world outside of baseball. At other times they were merely clever compositions, geared to the "Casey motif," but without much connection with "Casey" or his works.

THE BALL McCORMICK HIT

by Charles S. Taylor—1901

A deathlike hush had fallen, though excitement was intense,
On the crowd within the grandstand, and the boys upon the fence;
The "fans" packed on the bleachers held their breath as though afraid
They might disturb the quiet with the noise their breathing made.

Angry looks from angry thousands, on the Umpire too were cast,
And surely if they had their way, this game would be his last;
Two out, McCormick at the bat, the score stood three and three,
The pitcher smiled, spit on his hands and proudly bent his knee.

A whirl, a thrust, a cloud of dust, and forth the leather sped,
It shot by two feet from the plate, "one strike," the umpire said;
The crowd showed signs of anger, but with features firm yet mild,
McCormick, full of confidence, turned toward them all and smiled.

Again the pitcher grasped the ball, again his frame he bent,
And through the agitated air with lightning speed it went;
This time the ball went wider still, but the umpire called "strike two,"
The angry crowd surged to its feet, and the atmosphere was blue.

But mild McCormick smiled again to soothe the angry throng,
Then changed his bat for another that was heavy, smooth and long;

You could almost cut the quiet, it had grown so dense and thick,
As McCormick faced the pitcher, while he tightly grasped his stick.

One mighty swing, one fearful swat, and Mc had hit it fair,
And far above the fielder's head the ball sailed through the air;
Out into space it flew apace, a speck in heaven's dome,
While the crowd rushed madly toward the plate to meet Mc coming home.

Hip, hip for mild McCormick, long may he live and thrive,
The greatest batter in the world, the greatest one alive;
He saved the day for Punkville when on that outshoot he lit,
But the fielders never found the ball, the ball McCormick hit.

In a county just adjoining, in a pasture miles away,
With the hand of death upon her, a Holland heifer lay;
And grouped around in sorrow, with red and tearful eyes,
Were a dozen men commenting on the heifer's strange demise;
A frightful wound was in her side, and when they probed they found
A lump of something in her, all blood-stained, hard and round.

The country veterinary gave up the case because
He really wasn't satisfied "just what the darn thing was;"
He knew that "suthin' " killed her, and he thought that that was it,
But he never knew from then till now, 'twas the ball McCormick hit.[1]

As Napoleon Lajoie became recognized as one of the all-time greats of baseball, it was not surprising that his feats would be compared to those of "Mighty Casey." This verse was written on the eve of the 1907 season.

"MIGHTY LAJOIE" AND "MIGHTY CASEY"

by John F. Herne—1907

Years ago in cultured Boston there once strode up to the plate,
The renowned and mighty Casey who earned fame that lives to date;
In the bath he was an idol, very clever with the stick,
And its down on history's pages that that batsman was a Mick.

But time is ever on the wing and great people come and go,
As will the keystone sovereign, balldom's monarch pitchers' foe;
And of whom the wee boys prattle till at night they strike the hay,
And ere morning get to dreaming of Napoleon Lajoie.

Many are the times that Larry stung the artists of the slab,
Since he wandered from Woonsocket, where he piloted a cab;
By hitting clear across the fence more than once since he began,
To build up a reputation that made him the leading man.

He breaks up games in easy style with his varnished wagon tongue,
Just when you'd think the other side to their scalp belts had them hung;
And clinches victory then and there while the fans with glee do roar,
As he dashes round the bases and brings in the winning score.

Then for the gates they make a rush and you bet they cover ground,
When they beat it for the street cars full of joy and homeward bound.
And all proclaim in loudest tones there is no one like the king,
Till their cries are so far-reaching that they make the welkin ring.

On the corners every rooter, in the good old summer time,
From the Back Bay State to Frisco, and in every other clime;
Are telling how he wields the ash and gets ready for a slide,
When he's tearing down to second, as is the old horsehide.

It's the same all through the winter and New York can feel the jar,
For all biz is stopped in Wall Street when they mention this bright star;
He simply is the best there are, he is great, and that's enough,
And whoever found him surely got a diamond in the rough.

Flags will flaunt o'er graves of heroes that are yet to pass away,
And the nation's grandest pastime be just what it is today;
But big Larry nor poor Casey will be seen on field or bench,
Nor their prowess be forgotten by the Irish or the French.[2]

But Ty Cobb, enjoying his first great year, did much better than Lajoie in 1907, outhitting him .350 to .299 and leading the Detroit Tigers to their first American League title. The deciding game in the close pennant race between the Tigers and the Philadelphia Athletics took place in Philadelphia on September 30. Connie Mack's team trailed by one game in the standings and although each club had seven games remaining, their opposition was considered inferior and they were expected to win all of those contests.

The big game found Philadelphia leading 7–1 going into the seventh inning, and while the Tigers narrowed the gap, they still trailed 8–6 as the ninth inning began. At this point Ty Cobb homered off Rube Waddell with Sam Crawford on base to tie the score. The game went into extra innings. Detroit moved ahead 9–8 in the top of the eleventh, but the Athletics came back to even the score in their own half inning. On and on the teams battled. Darkness set in at the end of the seventeenth inning and the game was called with the score tied at 9. For Detroit the tie was as good as a win since the Tigers retained their one game advantage and the schedule favored them for the final week. They finished the season a game and one-half ahead of Philadelphia.[3]

Because of his ninth inning heroics, Cobb was the Detroit star. Harry Salsinger immortalized the deed in this fashion. (Unfortunately, the lines are garbled in the fifth stanza.)

TY COBB AT BAT

by Harry Salsinger—1907

It looked extremely rocky for the Tiger nine that day,
The score stood eight to six, with an inning left to play;
But Sam Crawford lined a single and brought suspense once more,
For Cobb, the mighty Tiger, was doping out the score.

There was ease in Ty Cobb's manner as he stepped into his place,
There was pride in Ty Cobb's bearing and a smile on Ty Cobb's face;
And, when responding to the silence, he tightly pulled his hat,
No stranger in the crowd could doubt 'twas Ty Cobb at the bat.

Eighty thousand eyes were on him as he rubbed his hands with dirt,
Forty thousand bit their lips when he wiped them on his shirt;
Then when the writhing Waddell ground the ball into his hip,
Defiance glanced in Ty Cobb's eye, a sneer curled Ty Cobb's lip.

But fame is fleeting as the wind and glory fades away,
There were no wild and woolly cheers, no glad acclaim this day;
They hissed and groaned and hooted as they clamored, "Strike him out!"
But Ty Cobb gave no outward sign that he had heard their shout.

The Reuben smiled and cut one loose,
Another hiss, another groan—"Strike one!" the umpire said;
No goading for the umpire now—his was an easy lot,
But when the Rube whirled round again—was that a rifle shot?
A whack! a crack! Through space the leather pellet flew,
A blot against the distant sky, a speck against the blue.

Above the fence in far right field, in rapid whirling flight,
The sphere sailed on, the blot grew dim and then was lost to sight;
Then forty thousand hearts were crushed, forty thousand threw a fit,
But none will ever find the ball that mighty Ty Cobb hit.

Oh, somewhere in this favored land the sun is shining bright,
The band is playing somewhere, and somewhere hearts are light;
And somewhere men are laughing where there never hangs a pall,
But there is no joy in Philly since mighty Tyrus hit that ball.[4]

It was noted earlier that many people thought Mike "King" Kelly, colorful
star of the 1880s and 1890s, was the prototype for "Casey."[5] Here is a poem
which glorified the "King's" base-running skills although spelling his name
differently.

LIKE KELLEY DID

by C. P. McDonald—1916

Bill Sweeney was a backstop on the mooted Bugville team,
At winging down to second base Bill Sweeney was a dream;
The rooters used to swear by him, he was their joy and pride,
Until he tried to emulate the famous ''Kelley Slide.''

For Bill had seen this Kelley steal base after base and slide,
Had noted carefully his work, his manner, and his stride;
And Sweeney wished a thousand ways each time the rooters cried,
They'd change the yell from Kelley and would screech, ''Slide, Sweeney, slide!''

But Kelley was a player with a wondrous burst of speed,
While Sweeney had a cracking whip but great speed seemed to need;
And though he copied Kelley's style, when possible, and slid,
The fans yelled: ''Sweeney stole a base! He did? Like Kelley did!''

For Sweeney was a moving van when e're he reached a bag,
And when he tried to steal, his feet would tangle up and lag;
And when he'd start, the fans would yelp together as a man,
''Oh, Sweeney, he can steal a base! He can? Like Kelley can!''

Now Sweeney was bullheaded, and he didn't seem to know
He hadn't speed enough to beat the slowest kind of throw;
But Sweeney said that Kelley stole a base each time he slid,
And so he'd keep on trying till he stole—like Kelley did!

The Captain used to argue, and he'd say: ''Now, look here, Bill,
You never yet ain't stole no base, and what's more, never will!
You're all right with your throwin' arm, and with the mitt you're rare,
But when it comes to pilferin' the bags, why, you ain't there!

''Now, this here Kelley's got a speed our whole team can't attain,
And how this bunch cops out the games is easy to explain;
But you—you've got to take a reef, put out your stealin' flames,
Because your wild cavortin's costin' us a lot of games!''

Well, Bill was decent for awhile and played a ripping game,
He curbed his strong ambition to perpetuate his name;
And when he safely stung the pill and galloped down to first,
He'd hug the sack so closely that the Captain raved and cursed.

But when the shades of evening fell and the moon rose o'er the hill,
Bill sneaked out to the baseball lot and stole the bags at will;
He'd take a long lead off of first, then slide upon his shirt,
For twenty feet, then stand on second and brush off the dirt.

At last the year drew to a close, the pennant season came,
And Bill was there behind the bat to play the final game;
"We'll take this fight," the Captain said to Bill, "and win the flag,
But for the love of all that's good, don't try to swipe a bag!"

The ninth round came, the visitors had tied the single score,
The side retired, the home boys came to bat amid a roar;
Bill opened with a double and was booted down to third,
Then rose the loudest rooting, Sweeney swore, he ever heard.

The next two died ere reaching first, and Bill was held on third,
Up stepped the heavy sticker of the team—a clouting bird;
But while Bill pawed the ground at third, out yelled a zealous fan:
"O, Bill can steal home base and win! He can? Like Kelley can!"

Bill heard! Before his eyes there flashed a swift and livid flame!
At last the time was come to act—immortalize his name!
His moonlight practice had improved his speed—he'd sure make good!
He now was fleet as Kelley and could steal—like Kelley could!

And then, e'en while the pitcher held the ball, Bill sprang from third!
"Go back, you bonehead," cried the boss, but Sweeney never heard;
A hush fell on the multitude—a silence deep, profound,
While Bill dived to the earth and plowed up twenty feet of ground!

In Bugville's potter's field today there is a little plot,
And o'er it stands a painted board which marks Bill's resting spot;
And those who run may read these words: "At last the fans are rid
Of Sweeney, who stole home and won! He did? Like Kelley did!"[6]

Frank Baker, the Philadelphia Athletics's third baseman, was another player
to be immortalized "Casey" fashion for his exploits. He won the second game
of the 1911 World Series with a two-run homer off "Rube" Marquard of the
New York Giants. The following day, with Christy Mathewson and the Giants
leading 1–0 in the top of the ninth, Baker tied the score with another home
run, a remarkable feat in those "dead ball" days. The Athletics won that game
in extra innings and went on to capture the World Series four games to two.
Forevermore, the slugger was known as "Home Run" Baker. Even before the
series was over, Grantland Rice had composed the following untitled verse:

They say that Casey had a punch before his Mudville rout,
They say that old Cap Anson once could line the leather out;
They speak of Keeler, Del and Flick, of Duffy and of Cobb,
Or chant the everlasting fame of Wagner on the job.

And while I have no knock for them, nor grudge them any fame,
Which they have earned with magic eye across a nation's game;
I'll tip my lid another way as war shouts rise and fall,
I'll back him up against the flock—when Baker hits the ball.[7]

A couple of months after the series was over, Baker's feat was glorified in more detailed fashion.

BAKER AT THE BAT

by W. Harry Heisler—1911

The outlook sure was dismal for Mack's great nine that day,
With the score at one to nothing and just one more round to play;
And then when Collins died at first and walked back with a frown,
There was gloom in every gesture of the fans from Quakertown.

The Gotham bugs were leaving, for they thought the game was won,
Didn't Matty, peerless Matty, have 'em stopped without a run?
Then a silent youth named Baker came to bat and toed the plate,
His eagle eye was gleaming and his batting poise was great.

But Matty, peerless Matty, had predicted what he'd do
To this same Baker fellow, for his weakness sure he knew;
There'd be no repetition of a ball knocked from the yard,
For 'twas Matty who was pitchin', not the rattle-brained Marquard.

So Matty, peerless Matty, signaled Meyers and touched his hat,
While he wound up for the "fade-away," with Baker at the bat;
The ball tore straight across the plate and Matty's grin was wide,
For the "fade-away" was workin'—"Strike one," the umpire cried.

"I'll sneak a fast one over now and make it number two,"
Thought Matty, as the horsehide toward the waiting Baker flew;
The rest is better left unsaid, 'tis sad when we recall
That over near the Polo Grounds they still hunt for that ball.

For Baker, mighty Baker, with a sure and deadly aim,
Has knocked another homer and the crowd has gone insane;
His teammates fall on Matty in another round or two,
And the game comes back to Philly, by a score of three to two.

Oh! somewhere they still sell gold bricks to simple country folk,
And love to spring that poor, old, worn out "sleeping city" joke;
And somewhere little "glooms" abide, while busy spielers hawk,
But they never mention Baker's name in little old Noo Yawk.

Oh! Casey, famous Casey, man who brought to Mudville fame,
Creature taught to us since childhood, but without an author's name;
You'll have to take a back seat now—and you'd best remove your hat,
For Baker, mighty Baker, "Home Run" Baker's at the bat.[8]

The 1920 season marked the beginning of the lively ball era and signaled the transition of baseball from a game of science and strategy to one of power-hitting. The age was heralded by George Herman "Babe" Ruth who, the year before, when hitting the dead ball, had already broken the single season home run record with twenty-nine circuit blows. He was with the Boston Red Sox that year. Moving to the New York Yankees in 1920, he took advantage of the "juiced-up" sphere and went on a home run binge which few followers of the game had dreamed possible. Ruth's new record of fifty-four homers for 1920 would be broken by himself the following year with fifty-nine. Already an established star, the Babe's home run feats had made him a national hero.

CASEY AT THE BAT—VERSION OF 1920

by Ed Van Every—1921

There was ease in Big Babe's manner and a large bat in his hand,
There was pride in Big Babe's bearing as he smiled and took his stand;
There was danger in his smiling as the pitcher made him wait,
It was easy to distinguish, it was Babe Ruth at the plate!

Sixty thousand eyes and eleven centered on the batsman rare,
Those odd numbered orbs are right folks, for a one-eyed guy was there;
Ah 'tis plain the nervous twirler now our slugger fears to face,
For the Babe is looking vicious—there's a man on second base.

Well, at last the sphere is hurtled, far it seems destined to ride,
But the Babe sneers with derision, for the ball is very wide;
"Boo!" and "Boo!" the great throng bellows. Some one yells, "Oh, where's my
    gun!"
And the fielders move out further as the umpire calls: "Ball one."

"Put it over," storm the rooters; once again the pitcher threw;
Louder shrieked the maddened thousands while the umpire called: "Ball two."
Closer to the plate edged Big Babe, he was mad as he could be,
And the crowd was fair demented as the umpire called "Ball three."

"Put it over!" "Put it over!" screamed the fans with faces red,
And you bet the pitcher tried to—put it over Big Babe's head;
For he knew with men on bases he must walk the King of Swat,
Ha! but Babe reached high and nailed that pitch and knocked it out the lot.

Oh, now this broad land over folks are grinning at the news,
And everywhere they're telling how the Babe baseballs can lose;
You bet the whole world's talking of each record breaking clout,
But there is no joy in Boston—Yep, Babe Ruth Made Another Homer Yesterday.[9]

In the wake of the Black Sox Scandal, where eight members of the powerful Chicago White Sox club were banished from baseball for allegedly conspiring to throw the 1919 World Series to the Cincinnati Reds, this untitled verse appeared in *The Sporting News*.

When mighty Casey fanned the air, as told by De Wolf Hopper,
The fans were an unhappy lot, and angry, too, old topper;
But now they have this cheery thought to take away the chill, oh!
For Casey, though he fanned, did not find cash beneath his pillow.[10]

Casey Stengel, a natural subject for "Casey" parodies, achieved poetic immortality on two different occasions, one as a player and one as a manager. In the 1923 World Series Stengel played center field for the New York Giants and his two home runs were instrumental in his club's two victories against the Yankees, in the third consecutive "subway series." The American Leaguers, however, won the series, four games to two. Babe Ruth led the Yankees with his prodigious hitting, which included three home runs. This was expected of Ruth, though, while Stengel's feats were a big surprise and won him great renown.

WHEN CASEY STENGEL CAME THROUGH

by Guy Lee—1923

It looked extremely rosy for the Yankees yesterday,
But, out in front, per usual, they kicked the game away;
They hobbled here and wobbled there and stumbled true to form,
And pretty soon were smothered 'neath a Giant slugging storm.

The Bimbo socked a triple and he never got past third,
And other smiling promises proved but a bust deferred;
But sixty thousand rooters cheered the Hugs with zeal and will,
For darn their blun'dring hides, with all their faults we love 'em still.

Aye, from the throats of that vast throng arose a frenzied roar,
When Bullet Bush and Jumping Joe combined and tied the score;
And hope was strong till in the ninth, with two guys leveled flat,
That cussed Casey Stengel came a-swarming up to bat.

O, somewhere in this bloomin' town there's fun and all that rot,
Somewhere are songs and gayety, in Harlem, like as not;
But over in the Bronx despair hangs as a pall,
For Casey, mighty Casey, knocked the cover off the ball.[11]

Grantland Rice composed a four-line verse on this unexpected event. He noted how the good and faithful Mudville fans had never abandoned their hero and concluded with a typical reaction when the news got back home: "Hey, I knew that good old Casey had it in him after all."[12]

Although the Washington Senators lost the 1925 World Series to Pittsburgh, four games to three (the Pirates made a spirited comeback after being down three games to one), the Washington left fielder Leon "Goose" Goslin became something of a hero for hitting three home runs. Joe "Moon" Harris, the Senators' right fielder, also hit three home runs and had a much higher batting average than Goslin, but no poem was written for him.

WHEN GOSLIN SOCKS THE BALL

by Gene Blossom—1925

You've always heard a lot of talk of Casey at the Bat,
Of how he'd often draw a walk, but kept his record fat;
He singled, doubled, tripled hard and still that wasn't all,
But hold tight to your whiskers, pard, when Goslin socks the ball!

Our friend Babe R. was pretty good a year or so ago,
He hit the leather with the wood and brought the pitchers woe;
To tell about the bustin' Bam I could go hire a hall,
But—listen to the hefty slam when Goslin socks the ball!

We're in a hole, three runs behind, some hurler going good,
To him Dame Fortune has been kind, our bunch has been his food;
McNeeley get a little hit, and Rice and Harris maul,
Then we go home and dream of it, when Goslin socks the ball![13]

Grover Cleveland Alexander, thirty-nine-year-old great, added laurels to his crown by his exceptional work in the 1926 World Series. He not only had been instrumental in helping the St. Louis Cardinals win the National League pennant, he also won two games and saved a third in the fall classic against the Yankees. He entered game seven in the seventh inning with his club leading by one run. Two men were out, the bases loaded, and young slugger Tony Lazzeri at bat. Lazzeri ripped a line drive foul to left and then proceeded to strike out a la "Casey." Alexander then shut the Yankees out over the last two innings to secure the game and the series. In his account of the game for the *New*

York Herald Tribune, Grantland Rice employed verse to mark Alexander's entrance into the game.

> There was ease in Aleck's manner as he shuffled to his place,
> There was pride in Aleck's bearing and a scowl on Aleck's face;
> And as he cut the first one through with speed that ever mocks,
> Not a rooter in the stands doubted 'twas Aleck in the box.[14]

Another football poem, "O'Toole's Touchdown," was recorded by De Wolf Hopper on the reverse side of a 1926 rendition of "Casey at the Bat." There is no information as to when this was written, nor was there a written version of it until Gardner included it in his anthology. O'Toole, the son of "Red" O'Toole, catcher on "Casey's" Mudville nine, bungled the situation worse than "Casey."

O'TOOLE'S TOUCHDOWN

by Les Desmond—1926

> The outlook wasn't brilliant for the Hokus team that day,
> The score was three to nothing with two minutes more to play;
> And so when Cohen lost five yards, and Zipkin did the same,
> A sickly silence fell upon the patrons of the game.
>
> A straggling few got up to go in deep despair, the rest
> Clung to the hope that springs eternal in the human breast;
> They thought if only Mike O'Toole was out there on the field,
> That fact might be enough to cause the other side to yield.
>
> But Mighty Mike O'Toole was out; his left arm had been broken,
> He hadn't been in any game since Hokus played Shemoken;
> So on that stricken multitude grim melancholy sat,
> A touchdown now would win the game, though who dared hope for that?
>
> But ten yards were gained by Cohen, to the wonderment of all,
> And Metza ran another ten before he downed the ball!
> And when the dust had lifted and they saw what had been done,
> Hokus was in midfield with but fifty yards to run!
>
> Then from five thousand throats and more went up a lusty yell,
> It rumbled in the valley, it rattled in the dell;
> It knocked upon the mountain top, and to the ear re-pealed,
> For O'Toole, Mighty Mike O'Toole, was trotting on the field!

There was ease in O'Toole's manner as he stepped into his place,
There was pride in O'Toole's bearing and a smile on O'Toole's face;
And when responding to the cheers he waved his good right palm,
No stranger doubted, 'twas O'Toole who stood there cool and calm.

Ten thousand eyes were on him as he dug his cleats in dirt,
Five thousand tongues applauded for they knew that he'd been hurt;
And as lower crouched the center, ready the ball to flip,
Defiance gleamed in O'Toole's eye, a sneer curled O'Toole's lip.

But ere the leather-covered ball came hurtling through the air,
O'Toole was leaping forward from his haughty grandeur there;
The whistle blew! Ole Hokus, five more yards was penalized,
Just that much farther from the goal, the thing so dearly prized.

From the benches black with people there went up a muffled roar,
Like the beating of the storm waves on a stern and distant shore;
"Kill that blamed official!" shouted someone on the stand,
And it's likely they'd have killed him had not O'Toole raised his hand.

With a smile of Christian charity great O'Toole's visage shone,
He stilled the rising tumult, he bade the game go on;
The line crouched low, the quarterback his rapid signals gave,
The ball snapped back, the line held firm, it didn't even cave.

But look! It is a forward pass from quarter to O'Toole!
The Mighty Mike has grabbed it; he has started for the goal!
With ball clutched firmly to his breast, he speeds with bound on bound,
He flies across the goal line, and then drops to the ground.

Oh, somewhere men are laughing, and children shout with glee,
And somewhere bands are playing, and somewhere hearts are free;
And somewhere in this favored land the glorious sun does shine,
But there is no joy in Hokus, O'Toole crossed the wrong goal line![15]

There had long been the feeling that New York City because of its large Jewish population needed a good Jewish baseball player. Finally, in the late 1920s the Giants came up with a promising young infielder, Andy Cohen, who was expected to fill the need. So enthusiastic were the Giants over Cohen's prospects that they traded superstar Rogers Hornsby to the Boston Braves in January 1928 for a couple of mediocrities. On opening day, April 11, the Braves came to the Polo Grounds and Cohen opposed Hornsby. Andy outshone "the Rajah" and earned the following accolade.

COHEN AT THE BAT

by Frank Getty—1928

The outlook wasn't cheerful for the Giants yesterday,
They were trailing by a run with but four innings left to play;
When Lindstrom flied to Richbourg and Terry weakly popped,
It looked as though those Bostons had the game as good as copped.

But Jackson smacked a single over Eddie Farrell's pate,
And Harper drew a pass because they feared him at the plate;
And from the stands and bleachers the cry of ''Oy, Oy'' rose
For up came Andy Cohen half a foot behind his nose.

There was ease in Bob Smith's manner and a smile on Hornsby's face,
For they figured they had Andy in the tightest sort of place;
It was make or break for Andy, while the fans cried ''Oy, Oy, Oy,''
And it wasn't any soft spot for a little Jewish boy.

And now the pitcher has the ball and now he lets it go
And now the air is shattered by the force of Casey's blow;
Well, nothing like that happened, but what do you suppose?
Why, little Andy Cohen socked the ball upon the nose.

Then from the stands and bleachers the fans in triumph roared,
And Andy raced to second and the other runner scored;
Soon they took him home in triumph, midst the blare of auto honks,
There may be no joy in Mudville, but there's plenty in the Bronx.[16]

One of the more unusual events in World Series history occurred in the fourth game of the 1941 classic between the Brooklyn Dodgers and the perennial American winner, the Yankees. New York led two games to one, but trailed 4–2 in the ninth inning with two out and no one on base. Hugh Casey, the Brooklyn pitcher, struck out Tommy Henrich, which should have ended the game and evened the series, but catcher Mickey Owen let the ball get past him and Henrich reached first base. With new life, the Yankees then scored four runs and won the game. The following day they took the series finale.

CASEY IN THE BOX

by Meyer Berger—1941

The prospects all seemed rosy for the Dodger nine that day,
Four to three the score stood, with one man left to play;
And so when Sturm died, and Rolfe the Red went out,
In the tall weeds in Canarsie you could hear the Dodgers shout.

A measly few got up to go as screaming rent the air. The rest
Were held deep-rooted by Fear's gnaw eternal at the human breast;
They thought with only Henrich, Hugh Casey had a cinch,
They could depend on Casey when things stood at the pinch.

There was ease in Casey's manner as he stood there in the box,
There was pride in Casey's bearing, from his cap down to his sox;
And when, responding to the cheers, he took up his trousers' sag,
No stranger in the crowd could doubt, he had them in the bag.

Sixty thousand eyes were on him when Casey toed the dirt,
Thirty thousand tongues applauded as he rubbed his Dodger shirt;
Then while the writhing Henrich stood a-swaying at the hip,
Contempt gleamed high in Casey's eye, a sneer curled Casey's lip.

And now the leather-covered sphere came hurtling through the air,
And Henrich stood awaiting it, with pale and frightened stare;
Close by the trembling Henrich the ball unheeded sped,
"He don't like my style," said Casey, "Strike One!" the umpire said.

From the benches black with people there went up a muffled roar,
Like the thunder of dark storm waves on the Coney Island shore;
"Get him!" "Get him, Casey!" shouted someone in the stand,
Hugh Casey smiled with confidence. Hugh Casey raised his hand.

With a smile of kindly charity Great Casey's visage shone,
He stilled the Faithful's screaming. He bade the game go on;
He caught Mickey Owen's signal. Once more the spheroid flew,
But Henrich still ignored it. The umpire bawled "Strike Two!"

"Yay!" screamed the maddened thousands, and the echo answered "Yay!"
But another smile from Casey. He held them under sway;
They saw his strong jaws tighten. They saw his muscles strain,
And they knew that Hughie Casey would get his man again.

Pale as the lily Henrich's lips; his teeth were clenched in hate,
He pounded with cruel violence his bat upon the plate;
And now Great Casey held the ball, and now he let it go,
And Brooklyn's air was shattered by the whiff of Henrich's blow.

But Mickey Owen missed this strike. The ball rolled far behind,
And Henrich speeded to first base, like Clipper on the wind;
Upon the stricken multitude grim melancholy perched,
Dark disbelief bowed Hughie's head. It seemed as if he lurched.

DiMaggio got a single. Keller sent one to the wall,
Two runs came pounding o'er the dish and, oh, this wasn't all;

For Dickey walked, and Gordon a resounding double smashed,
And Dodger fans were sickened. All Dodger hopes were bashed.

O somewhere north of Harlem the sun is shining bright,
Bands are playing in the Bronx and up there hearts are light;
In Hunt's Point men are laughing, on The Concourse children shout,
But there is no joy in Flatbush. Fate has knocked their Casey out.[17]

In the year following the end of World War II the country was beset by a
series of labor disputes which slowed the readjustment of the economy from
wartime to peacetime. All of the trouble prompted H. I. Phillips of the *New
York Sun* to compose the following verse. Among the characters mentioned,
Truman, of course, was president, Louis Schwellenbach was secretary of labor,
John Steelman was the federal mediator, and Claude Pepper was then a senator
from Florida, although he later became a member of the House of Representatives.

MODERN CASEY AT THE BAT

by H. I. Phillips—1946

The outlook wasn't brilliant for the Mudville nine that day,
The score stood four to two, with but one inning more to play;
And so when Cooney died at first and Barrows did the same,
A sickly silence fell upon the patrons of the game.

A straggling few got up to go in deep despair; the rest
Clung to the hope that springs eternal in the human breast;
They thought, if only Casey but could get a whack at that,
They'd put up even money now, with Casey at the bat.

But Flynn was out on unpaid dues and Blake was out because
The local had convicted him of breaking union laws;
So upon that stricken multitude grim melancholy sat,
For it seemed it might take Truman to get Casey to the bat.

But mediators gathered, and they handed down the word,
To put a man on second and assign a sub to third;
The players raised a protest but in time they said, "Okay,
It's better than to have the Army in upon the play."

Then from the gladdened multitude went up a joyous yell,
It bounded from the mountain top and rattled in the dell;
It struck upon the hillside, and recoiled upon the flat,
For Casey, Mighty Casey, was advancing to the bat.

Ten thousand eyes were on him as he rubbed his hands with dirt,
And wiped them, by the rule book, upon his union shirt;
As Local Thirty's hurler ground the ball into his hip,
Defiance gleamed in Casey's eye, a sneer curled Casey's lip.

And now the leather-covered sphere came hurtling through the air,
As Casey raised a banner with the printed word, "Unfair";
Close by the sturdy batsman the ball unheeded sped,
"Enslaver," muttered Casey, "Strike one," the umpire said.

"Kill him! Kill the umpire!" shouted some one in the stand,
But Casey bade them "Silence, a fact-finding board's at hand";
"Conspiracy," thought Casey, but a smile upon him shone,
He stilled the rising tumult, he bade the game go on;
He signaled to the pitcher and once more the spheroid flew,
But Casey still ignored it, and the umpire said "Strike two!"

His teammates from the dugout rushed with angry cries of "Fraud,"
(Now Schwellenbach was frightened stiff and Truman, too, was awed);
Fact-finders huddled quickly, Steelman leaped into the breach,
And somewhere in the distance Pepper made another speech.

Oh, somewhere in this distraught land, the sun is shining bright,
The band is playing somewhere, and somewhere hearts are light;
And somewhere men are laughing and somewhere children shout,
But there is no joy in Mudville, Mighty Casey has walked out![18]

In the bottom of the eighth inning of the seventh and deciding game of the 1946 World Series the score was tied at three between the homestanding St. Louis Cardinals and the visiting Boston Red Sox. Enos Slaughter, leading off for St. Louis, singled to center, but Whitey Kurowski popped out trying to bunt and Del Rice flew out to Ted Williams. Harry Walker then hit safely to left center field, sending Slaughter to third. When Boston shortstop Johnny Pesky held the relay throw from the outfield too long, Slaughter continued on running and scored the run which won the game and the series.

SLAUGHTER AT THE BAT

by Joseph Farrell—1947

It looked extremely rocky for the Redbird team that day,
The Series stood at three games apiece—one game remained to play;
The fans of old St. Louis had the jitters as they sat,
And worried every time the mighty Williams came to bat.
They feared the wiles of Cronin who was cultured through and through,

And ran his team like coaches of old Harvard College do;
His language in the dressing room would put Shakespeare to rout,
And oftentimes his phrases left the Red Sox minds in doubt.
For instance, to his hurlers he would speak in accents tense,
"Proceed out to the mound, my lad, and hurl with vehemence."
Or to a batter he would say " 'Tis time to navigate,
And pound with cruel violence your bat upon the plate;
And when the spheroid reaches you, then with prodigious might
Propel the leathered apple like a rocket in its flight."

And so the afternoon wore on until they reached the eighth,
And fans of old St. Louis in God they put their faith;
The score was tied at three apiece and Slaughter was at bat,
When Cronin strolled out to the mound to Klinger for a chat.
In Harvard tones he spoke to Bob, for Joe was Bahston bred,
"Just speed one at his cranium and he'll drop dead," he said;
And now the leather-covered sphere came hurtling through the air,
And Slaughter met it squarely and it sailed to center, fair.
Then from the gladdened multitude went up a joyous yell,
It rumbled on the mountain tops, it rattled in the dell;
It struck upon the hillside and rebounded on the flat,
And everyone was wondering what Joe would say to that.

Then Cronin, mighty Cronin, with his cultured Boston air,
Meandered to the mound and posed in grandeur there;
Defiance gleamed in Cronin's eye, a snarl curled Cronin's lip,
And then in tones staccato, like the cracking of a whip,
Said haughty Cronin to his men who gathered at the plate,
"Now is the time to show these folks we rank among the great.
Return to all your posts, my braves, and let me run the game,
And I shall guide each one of you to everlasting fame."

There was ease in Cronin's manner as he made the throng believe
That he was cunning to the core with something up his sleeve;
And well they might believe the worst, for soon two men were out,
But Walker of St. Louis caused the mighty crowd to shout.
He looped a Texas Leaguer and Johnny Pesky turned his back,
And Slaughter started off from first to reach the second sack;
And Pesky then received the ball and should have thrown to third,
For Slaughter now was running with the fleetness of a bird.
Joe Cronin dashed out to the line as though shot from a gun,
And glared at Pesky who was watching Slaughter on the run;
Then Cronin's Harvard accent rose, his words were heard by all,
"Pesky, Pesky, Pesky, for gosh sake trow da ball!"

Oh, somewhere in this favored land the sun is shining bright,
The band is playing somewhere, and somewhere hearts are light;
And somewhere men are laughing, and somewhere children call,
But there is no joy in Boston since Pesky held the ball.[19]

Casey Stengel made his second appearance in the "Casey" literature in 1952 as he managed the New York Yankees to their third consecutive world championship. The victims, again, were the Brooklyn Dodgers.

CASEY AT THE BAT—'52 VERSION

by Karl Hubenthal—1953

The outlook wasn't brilliant for the Yankee nine that day,
The series score stood three and three with one game left to play;
There was concern in Casey's manner as he paced the dugout floor,
His Yanks were champs—three in a row, this *must* be number four!

The Bums had tied it in the fourth, the fifth inning was the same,
But Mantle's bat in the sixth and seventh, finally sewed up the game;
Lopat, Reynolds, Raschi—Kuzava, almost everyone but Sain,
Had trod the mound while Dodger bats kept swinging all in vain.

So somewhere in this favored land there is the gloom of night,
The band is muted somewhere and somewhere there is blight;
And somewhere men are weeping and somewhere there is pain,
That somewhere is in Flatbush, Cagey Casey's won again![20]

The amazing performance of the New York Mets—a 1962 expansion team, which had been the worst club in modern baseball—in winning the 1969 National League pennant and then defeating Baltimore to win the world championship, had to be graven in verse. On the eve of the series, as the team waited at LaGuardia Airport to board a United Airlines chartered flight to Baltimore, the proud mayor of New York, John Lindsay, stepped forward and recited this "Ode to the New York Mets."

Oh, the outlook isn't pretty for the Orioles today,
They may have won the pennant, but the Mets are on the way;
And when Gil Hodges's supermen get through with Baltimore,
They'll be the champions of the world—they'll win it in all four.

The experts say they cannot win, but they'll just eat their words,
When Jones and Koos and Agee pluck the feathers off those Birds;
When Gentry shuts out Robinson and Ryan does the same,
The world will know the Mets have come to dominate the game.

With Harrelson and Kranepool, with Gaspar and with Weis,
With Grote, Shamsky, Boswell—we've got the game on ice;
And when we've got a manager like Gilbert Raymond Hodges,
We've got a team that makes up for the Giants and the Dodge's.

So good luck down in Baltimore, New Yorkers place your bets,
We know we've got a winner—with our Amazin' Mets.[21]

On the eve of the 1975 World Series between Cincinnati and Boston, Senator Edward Kennedy, Democrat from Massachusetts, rose on the floor of the United States Senate and submitted a resolution which was passed by a voice vote. The resolution commended both clubs as the best in baseball and hoped each would win all the games played on its home field. Four games were scheduled (if necessary) in Boston, three in Cincinnati. Following the series, which Cincinnati won, four games to three, John Glenn, former astronaut and then Democratic senator from Ohio, arose and addressed the chamber.

ODE TO THE SERIES '75

by John Glenn—1975

'Twas 3 to 2 the Series stood at Riverfront that day,
With next the move to Boston, and two games left to play;
There was ease in Boston's manner as they homed on Fenway Park,
With its left field Green-wall Monster looming awesome, drear and stark.

The Gods of Sport who knew in full of what was going to be,
Then cried such tears it flooded all, for days that numbered three;
But even Gods must dry their tears when Series time comes nigh,
The rain stopped falling—field was dried, all under bright blue sky.

"Play Ball" the blue-coat umpire said and batters strode to plate,
As inning after inning passed with baseball simply great;
The Fenway ballpark rocked and roared as Red Sox hit quite free,
And when the dust had settled down the Series stood three-to-three.

The seventh game, that fateful night, tomorrow won't be there,
With Series tied at even up, both clubs threw way all care;
At inning nine the score was tied and still the battle roared,
But class will out, Joe Morgan hit, drove in the winning score.

Oh, somewhere in this favored land the sun is shining bright,
The band is playing somewhere, and somewhere hearts are light;
But Boston's men aren't laughing, and children don't dare to shout,
For there is no joy in Boston, the mighty Red Sox are all out.

Cincinnati wins the crown—a toast, they got their due,
But another toast to Boston, for they're true champions, too;
They played a hard and skillful game, they played it straight, no tricks,
We wish them well, minus Indians's games, in 1976.

To the Senior Senator from Mass., his hopes so sadly smote,
We point out Senate limits of quiet-passed "voice votes";
The "ayes" and "nays" for next year's moves, I call for here today,
That's just in case these two great teams may next year's Series play.

A serious note to end this tome, such excellence, rare-made,
It's been great pleasure just to watch these craftsmen ply their trade;
If every effort in this land had dedication same,
Perhaps our problems would grow small—a lesson from these games.[22]

In a 1972 National Football League divisional playoff game the Pittsburgh Steelers defeated the Oakland Raiders on an incredible play. Terry Bradshaw's pass bounced crazily off an Oakland defender's knee about fifteen yards backward into the unexpecting hands of ace running back Franco Harris. Harris carried the ball into the end zone for an important score. This untitled verse by Joe Bennett described the unusual play.

The outlook wasn't rosy on that bleak December day,
The Steelers, trailing 7–6, were sixty yards away;
Less than a minute now remained for Pittsburgh's eager team,
To cross that deadly battleground and keep alive their dream.
Among the fifty thousand there, a deep despair swelled then,
Could even Franco save the day, when it was fourth and ten?
And so, they called one last time-out—the Raiders crouched to wait,
Across the line of battle, then, they glared with savage hate.
And now, young Bradshaw calls the play—he signals for the ball,
The Raiders launch a desperate charge against the Steeler wall;
A copper pellet arcs its way across the graying sky,
Two men rush grimly under it, they meet and then a sigh
Drifts from the stricken multitude—the ball has bounded clear,
Already that familiar growl is heard: "Wait 'til next year";
But like a spirit from the air, a great brown savior flies,
And plucks with fine Italian hands the ball, before it dies.
Oh, somewhere in this troubled land, the clouds hang grim and low,
And hearts are heavy somewhere, and somewhere cold winds blow;
And somewhere men are weeping, and somewhere fans are blue,
But that somewhere isn't Pittsburgh, for mighty Franco has come through.[23]

In the second game of the 1978 World Series between those ancient rivals, the Los Angeles Dodgers and the New York Yankees, the Yankees trailed with two out and two on in the top of the ninth. Los Angeles's young fire-baller Bob Welch faced the Yankee slugger Reggie Jackson. After working the count to three-and-two, Jackson fouled off the next three pitches.

. . . AND THE MIGHTY REGGIE HAS STRUCK OUT

by Jules Loh—1978

The outlook wasn't brilliant for the Yankees in L.A.,
The score stood 4–3, two out, one inning left to play;
But when Dent slid safe at second and Blair got on at first,
Every screaming Dodger fan had cause to fear the worst.

For there before the multitude—Ah destiny! Ah fate!
Reggie Jackson, mighty Reggie, was advancing to the plate;
Reggie, whose three home runs had won the year before,
Reggie, whose big bat tonight fetched every Yankee score.

On the mound to face him stood the rookie, young Bob Welch,
A kid with a red hot fastball—Reggie's pitch—and nothing else;
Fifty thousand voices cheered as Welch gripped ball in mitt,
One hundred thousand eyes watched Reggie rub his bat and spit.

"Throw your best pitch, kid, and duck," Reggie seemed to say,
The kid just glared. He must have known this wasn't Reggie's day;
His first pitch was a blazer. Reggie missed it clean,
Fifty thousand throats responded with a Dodger scream.

They squared off, Reggie and the kid, each knew what he must do,
And seven fastballs later, the count was three and two;
No shootout on a dusty street out here in the Far West,
Could match the scene; a famous bat, a kid put to the test.

One final pitch. The kid reared back and let a fastball fly,
Fifty thousand Dodger fans gave forth one final cry;
Ah, the lights still shine on Broadway, but there isn't any doubt,
The Big Apple has no joy left. Mighty Reggie has struck out.[24]

In the following World Series a remarkable relief pitching performance was turned in by Kent Tekulve of the Pittsburgh Pirates. The Pirates won the series four games to three and Tekulve earned "saves" in three of the four wins. A 1969 graduate of Marietta College, "Teke" was honored by the city of Marietta and the college after the season was over. December 8, 1979, was designated "Kent Tekulve Day" and festivities were concluded with a banquet that night on the campus.

The author, who had done some "versifying" on local themes, was invited by the committee to compose a poem-tribute to the college's most distinguished athlete-alumnus. Concentrating on the seventh game—and modifying the poem for present purposes—this is what he wrote and recited at the banquet.

ONE COOL OCTOBER NIGHT

by Gene Murdock—1979

The prospect was uncertain for the Fam-a-lee that night,
Three men were on, two men were out, that one run lead was slight;
The final game, the chips were down, the bundle on the line,
The top, the peak, the summit, now called the Pirate nine.

The trail was long, the journey hard, but success was close at hand,
Having won the East and trounced the West, they neared the Promised Land;
But slugging Eddie Murray, in the left hand batter's place,
Could spoil the plot and wreck the scene, with his mighty home run mace.

Astride the hill in perfect calm, the thin man eyed the plate,
His task was clear, his job laid out, he let the roar abate;
He rocked and fired the sinker pitch, "Ball One," was the cry,
The crowd stood up and cheered their man, and acclaimed his careful eye.

Teke stepped up, surveyed the scene and fired again at Murray,
Eddie took the pitch, so fast and true, he was in no great hurry;
But the audience was angry as the umpire called "Strike One,"
They craved a walk, a hit, a balk, just get that tying run.

The count was even up at one, Teke wound again and threw,
The ball was just outside the plate, on the mound the air was blue;
The roar this time crescendoed, the fans they all went wild,
They'd little reason to suspect, he had them all beguiled.

Once more two-seven made his pitch—a hummer low and hard,
It cut the plate above the knees, caught Murray off his guard;
Then from the benches black with people arose a mighty boo,
For the man in blue behind the plate had called the pitch "Strike Two."

The count now stands at two-and-two, Tekulve wheels and deals,
Murray strokes it deep to right, big Dave turns on the wheels;
He slips and nearly hits the ground, but soon regains his balance,
In tracking down that hard-hit ball, he showed the world his talents.

The Orioles had missed a chance, there's one inning more to go,
Can Teke maintain his mastery? Soon we all shall know;
In the top half of that inning, the Buccos played inspired,
Two more Pirates crossed the plate 'fore three had been retired.

Only three outs still remain until that glorious great moment,
The Orioles can't be allowed, a rally big to foment;
Our hero is compelled to use his skill, his brains, his get-up,
No slips, no errors, no mistakes, no momentary let-up.

Young Roenicke strode to the plate, a strong right-handed hitter,
Would that Teke knew how to throw the long prohibited spitter;
But his sinker was sufficient, he uncorked those three straight strikes,
A masterful achievement, of which few had seen the likes.

Next came Doug DeCinces and as he strolled up to his place,
He was a-shakin' and a-sweatin', defeat writ on his face;
Three pitches more came plateward, all were low and away,
The great truth dawned on Dougie D., that this was not his day.

Last hope for the Orioles was Kelly, pinch-hitter supreme,
The Pirates had to stop him, to be the title team;
Pat hit to left, Pat hit to center, Pat could also hit to right,
And when Pat hit he'd always hit with every ounce of might.

Now on the verge of vict'ry, Teke to Madlock said "Man,
It's the out we have awaited since spring training first began";
The battle was quite brief for Kelly popped up in the middle,
Omar Moreno moved in fast and shrilled, "Hi-diddle-diddle."

The Pirate team erupted, they had reached their cherished goal,
Oh, how they screamed; Oh, how they hugged: they gloried in their role;
The clubhouse was in chaos, there was Teke and Starge and Bowie,
Even Jimmy Carter had his say—no doubt a lot of hooey.

In the pantheon of heroes, Marietta has had its share,
Rufus Putnam, Dean Hess, Dawes, you can see them all up there;
But no searchlight ever shown with such a brilliant light,
As it did on Kent Tekulve, on that cool October night.[25]

10.

Leftovers

The remaining verses in the "Casey" literature do not fit in any particular category so they are brought together here. They may deal with Mudville, or they may casually mention "Casey," or they may speak of "Casey's"—and Hopper's—eternal glory. A "Casey" in black dialect, as well as a version in the "mod" language of the 1950s, also find refuge here.

Grantland Rice was the only writer who was concerned much about the future of the village of Mudville after "Casey's" strikeout, although his feelings on the subject were ambivalent. He wrote three poems with a reference to Mudville either in the title or in the substance of the work. His central point was that within twenty-five years after the mighty miss, the town disappeared from the map. This was rather strange because in his first revision of "Casey's Revenge" Rice told of a monument to our hero which had been built in Mudville's public square.

MUDVILLE'S FATE

by Grantland Rice—1910

I wandered back to Mudville, Tom, where you and I were boys,
And where we drew in days gone by our fill of childish joys;
Alas! the town's deserted now, and only rank weeds grow,
Where Mighty Casey fanned the air just twenty years ago.

Remember Billy Woodson's place where, in the evening's shade,
The bunch would gather and discuss the home runs Casey made;
Dog fennel now grows thick around that "joint" we used to know,
Before old Casey whiffed the breeze some twenty years ago.

The grandstand, too, has been torn down; no bleachers met my gaze,
Where you and I were wont to sit in happy bygone days;

The peanuts which we fumbled there have sprouted in a row,
Where Mighty Casey swung in vain just twenty years ago.

O how we used to cheer him, Tom, each time he came to bat!
And how we held our breath in awe when on the plate he spat;
And when he landed on the ball, how loud we yelped! But Oh,
How loud we cursed when he struck out some twenty years ago.

The diamond is a corn patch now; the outfield's overgrown
With pumpkin vines and weedy plots; the rooters all have flown—
They couldn't bear to live on there, for nothing was the same,
Where they had been so happy once before that fatal game.

The village band disbanded soon, the mayor, too, resigned,
The council even jumped its graft, and in seclusion pined;
The marshal caught the next train out, and those we used to know,
Began to leave in flocks and droves some twenty years ago.

For after Casey fanned that day the citizens all left,
And one by one they sought new lands, heartbroken and bereft;
The joyous shout no more rang out of children at their play,
The village blacksmith closed his shop, the druggist moved away.

Alas for Mudville's vanished pomp when Mighty Casey reigned!
Her grandeur has departed now; her glory's long since waned;
Her place upon the map is lost, and no one seems to care
A whit about the old town now since Casey biffed the air.[1]

Three years after writing "Mudville's Fate," Rice composed another verse practically identical with it, although he made a few changes, and he dedicated the piece to De Wolf Hopper.

TO DE WOLF ("IMMORTAL CASEY") HOPPER

by Grantland Rice—1913

I wandered back to Mudville, Hop, where you and I were boys,
And where we drew, in days gone by, our fill of youthful joys;
Alas! the town's deserted now, and only rank weeds grow,
Where mighty Casey fanned the air just twenty years ago.

Remember Billy Woodson's place, where in the evening's shade,
The old bunch gathered to discuss the home runs Casey made?
Dog fennel now grows thick around that joint we used to know,
Before old Casey biffed the breeze some twenty years ago.

The grandstand, too, has been torn down; no bleachers met my gaze,
Where you and I were wont to sit in happy bygone days;

The peanuts which we fumbled there have sprouted in a row,
Where mighty Casey swung in vain just twenty years ago.

Oh, how we used to cheer him, Hop, each time he came to bat,
And how we held our breath in awe as on the plate he spat;
And when he landed on the ball, how loud we yelled—but O—
How loud we cursed when he struck out those twenty years ago.

The diamond is a corn patch now; the outfield's overgrown
With pumpkin vines and weedy plots; the rooters all have flown—
They couldn't bear to linger there when you in that dim age,
Exploded Mudville's awful jolt each night upon the stage.

The village band disbanded soon; the mayor, too, resigned,
The council even jumped its graft, and in seclusion pined;
The marshal caught the next train out, and those we used to know
Began to leave in flocks and droves some twenty years ago.

For after Casey fanned that day the town began to slump,
The wild-eyed fans no longer met around the village pump;
The joyous shouts no more rang out of children at their play,
The village blacksmith closed his shop; the druggist moved away.

Alas for Mudville's vanished pomp when mighty Casey reigned!
Her grandeur has departed now; her glory's long since waned;
Her place upon the map is lost, and no one seems to care,
Since Casey, in that famous pinch, stepped up—and biffed the air.[2]

Rice's final Mudville verse had little to do with Mudville's fate as expressed
in the previous two poems. This referred to a series of crippling injuries which
had beset the town's team. But apparently a number of major league clubs were
experiencing this difficulty, and Mudville merely symbolized them all.

MUDVILLE'S FATE UPDATED

by Grantland Rice—1912

"The outlook wasn't brilliant for the Mudville nine that year,"
Big Casey has a broken leg which tightened up his gear;
And Kelley's spine was fractured, and Flynn's right arm was lame,
"So a sickly silence fell upon the patrons of the game."

The shortstop had a busted knee, and Zeke a shattered neck,
Six members of the outfield and the infield were a wreck;
The team's four leading pitchers writhed in pain upon a cot,
While the ambulance was skidding in a whirl around the lot.

"O, somewhere in this favored land the sun is shining bright,"
Somewhere a bloke has two good arms and both his legs are right;
But Mudville has the habit now, from leading star to dub,
Where the bat boy is the only guy in shape to swing a club.[3]

In spite of Grantland Rice's efforts to expunge Mudville from the map, the town was still prospering in 1918, and the fans still turned out, even though that was a bad year for baseball.

THE HOLD-OUT

Anonymous–1918

February 16

"I will not play this season," said shortstop Eddie Brown,
"I hit two-eighty eight last year, now Mudville cuts me down;
I fielded just like Maranville and never missed a play,
I think, b'gee! instead of less they ought to raise my pay."

March 16

"They're starting on the training trip, but darned ef I c'n go,
I'll never move a step down South until I get the dough;
But then—perhaps—they *will* come through 'n I might not be there,
I guess I'll string 'long with the boys an' get that Texas air."

April 16

The Mudville crowd is silent now, the other nine's ahead,
Two men are out, the bags are full, our hearts half hope, half dread;
Who is it hooks that fast one o'er the fence and wins the game?
Five thousand throats are telling you—why, Shortstop Brown—the same![4]

Another group of "Casey" verses merits inclusion simply because of an offhand reference to the mighty one, or at least what appears to be such a reference. In this ballad, Mooney is the slugger, not "Casey," but our hero herein demonstrates a skill not before recognized.

WHEN MOONEY STINGS THE BALL

Anonymous—1910

When Murphy bunts and gets to first, we cheer his feat with pride,
The ball twists slowly down the line, and never rolls outside;
When Casey makes a sacrifice, his deftness moves us all,
But, oh, the real hi-hi-ing comes, when Mooney stings the ball!

For Mooney has a nervous way of handling his bat,
The pitchers hate to watch his eyes, they don't know where they are at;
He stands there ready with the stick, upon the sphere to fall,
And, oh, the crowd lets out a yell when Mooney stings the ball.

Yes, Mooney was designed by fate, to make the pitchers mourn,
The foxy inshoots and the wides, he lets pass by with scorn;
He stands regardless of the crowd, the strikes, the umpires call,
Until the sphere floats o'er the plate—then Mooney stings the ball.

It moves us when the center field pulls down the fly he's cursed,
It thrills us when the shortstop's throw cuts off a man at first;
But, oh, the fierce excitement when, the bases filled, we all
Leap up and howl, and dance, and yell, when Mooney stings the ball.[5]

With his training in the classics, Grantland Rice frequently invoked the lessons of ancient history to bring modern sports into perspective.

SOME BASEBALL REMINISCENCES

by Grantland Rice—1909

Old Noah was a Baseball Bug of thirty-third degree,
He seldom ever missed a game in his vicinity;
And have you heard why Noah sailed one morning in the Ark?
He'd gotten tired of postponed games from water in the park.

And there was old Methuselah—another wild eyed fan,
He lived nine hundred years or more before he chopped the span;
He lived to this extended age by feeding on the hope,
That Cleveland would some distant day play up to April's dope.

Alas, for poor old Socrates, another ancient Bug;
I wonder if you've heard just why he hit the "Hemlock jug."
Nine bad defeats for Athens was a blow to luckless Soc.,
But when she dropped her "fourteen straight" he couldn't stand the shock.

You've heard of Bill Diogenes, the lantern-toting guy,
Who went from place to place and peered with eagle eye;
The story as I got it from a fellow who was there,
Is that old Diog was hunting for an umpire on the square.

J. Caesar was the Casey of the days of long ago—
He led the league in batting by a dozen miles or so;
But, like the Mighty Casey, one day Caesar swung and missed,
They struck him out and left his name upon the Mudville list.

The score was tied—the fourteenth round had started—when, alack,
The daylight started glimmering and shadows gathered black;
And that's why Mogul Joshua, to score the winning run,
Sent in his famous wireless, "Don't hurry," to the sun.[6]

"Casey's" cousin in this poem was no blood relative of Mighty Casey. Here "cousin" appears to be used in the baseball sense where the batter, usually an easy out for a particular pitcher, is that pitcher's "cousin."

CASEY'S COUSIN AT THE BAT

by C.P.S.—1915

Were you ever on the bleachers when the game was nearly done,
With the home team coming into bat and in need of one big run?
Did you notice how the anxious ones went toward the nearest gate,
And when the leadoff man got on, they'd stop right there and wait.

And when the next man bunted how they edged back just a bit,
Hoping that the third one would come through and make a hit;
And how they dropped their jaws when he was thrown out at first,
It seemed to them the home team's luck was of the very worst.

One on third and two men out and yet they all remain,
Hoping still for the timely hit that now would tie the game;
The mighty Casey of the team is coming to the plate,
And the fans stand up and yell aloud, "Ol' man, it ain't too late!"

Well, this Casey didn't strike out, nor he didn't make a hit,
But he popped the first ball pitched to him right in the shortstop's mitt.[7]

Like "Casey's" cousin, Hickey did not strike out, but he also failed to come through when the home team hopes were riding with him.

UP CAME HICKEY

Anonymous—1923

Three runners perched upon the bags,
One out the scoreboard said;
The enemy was one run up,
And eight lone rounds had sped.
"We have a chance," the pilot cried,
"That Hickey knocks it dead."

This Hickey was no Mudville star,
No Casey at the bat;

He was not one to fan the air
And leave the home town flat—
Not Hickey, he was guilty of
A much worse crime than that.

"Ball one," the umpire shouted clear,
"Just throw the ball my way,"
Said Hickey to the pitcher meek,
"And watch me win the day."
He grooved one and our Hickey hit—
Into a double play.[8]

It was to be expected that before too long a version of "Casey" would appear in black dialect.

MISTAH CASEY DONE STRUCK OUT

by John Thornton—1908

I know dem Mudville fellows wouldn't win dat day fur sho',
Dey only had one run you know, dem other folks had fo';
Dey only had one round to go an' two de bes' men down,
Dat was de sickes' lookin' bunch you'd find in any town.

Dem fellows in de fo' bit seats got up to go away,
De bleachers an' dem what climed de fence made up dere minds to stay;
Dey said if Mistah Casey got a lick dare'd be some fun,
He'd knock dat ball clean out o' sight, an' make de winnin' run.

Two easy mutts was on de lis' fo' Mistah Casey, though,
Dey said de odds was fo' to one dat Mudville wouldn't show;
I didn't have a single buck to put down either way,
A little game de night befo' cleaned up my whole week's pay.

But one dem muts got on de base, jes how, I done forgit,
De other slam de ball out hard, an' den git up an' git;
An' when de bunch seen what was done, an' two men on de base
Dey jes got up an' acted like dey's gwine to wreck de place.

Dey set up sich a holler, you could hear it on de moon,
Dey said dey'd win the game now, an' dey'd win it mighty soon;
Fuh Mistah Casey he was nex', he looked so fine and proud,
He turned aroun' and tetched his cap, an' den politely bowed.

De people cheered an' cheered agin, dey told him he was it,
Dey said "go fuh him Casey an' make a fo'-base hit."

De pitcher den got ready, den he throwed de ball,
But Mistah Casey didn't seem to like dat kind at all.

One strike de umpire hollered, an' den dat crowd broke loose,
I never heard sich cussin' or sich terrible abuse;
One fellow said we'll kill him, another say you bet,
But Mistah Casey smiled an' said, "Dis game ain't over yet."

Den de pitcher squared himself an' throwed agin you know,
But Mistah Casey said it was about a foot too low;
Two strikes de umpire hollered, an' den it 'peared to me,
Dere was gwine to be a funeral, jes as sure as sure could be.

Dey 'bused dat umpire scanlous, called him every kind o' name,
Dey said he was a lemon what didn't know de game;
Dey said some things I think I better not recall,
Dey wouldn't sound quite proper, no, dey wouldn't do at all.

De nex' ball which de pitcher throwed, looked crooked as a snake,
An' Mistah Casey said I've got dat fo' base hit to make;
He drawed his bat way up, an' he made a mighty swing,
He hurt his arm an' sprained his back, but didn't do a thing.

I spec de sun is shinin' somewhar in de land,
I spec de folks is list'ning to de playin' 'f de band;
I spec de children hab some fun, I spec dey run and shout,
But not aroun' in Mudville, Mistah Casey done struck out![9]

In 1960 the editors of *Mad Magazine*, a monthly journal of satire, cartoons, and nonsense, published their own version of "Casey," employing the jargon of the day.

COOL CASEY AT THE BAT

by Editors of *Mad Magazine*—1960

The action wasn't groovy for the Endsville nine that day,
The beat was 4 to 2 with just one chorus more to sway;
And when old Cooney conked at first, and Barrows also sacked,
A nowhere rumble bugged up all the cats who dug the act.

A hassled group got all hung up and started in to split,
The other cats there played it cool and stayed to check the bit;
They figured if old Casey could, like, get in one more lick,
We'd put a lot of bread down, Man, on Casey and his stick!

But Flynn swung before Casey, and also Cornball Blake,
And the first stud didn't make it, and the other couldn't fake;
So the cats and all their chicks were dragged and in a bluesy groove,
For it was a sucker's long-shot that old Casey'd make his move.

But Flynn blew one cool single, and the hipsters did a flip,
And Blake, who was a loser, gave the old ball quite a trip;
And when the tempo let up, like a chorus played by Bird,
There was Cornball stashed at second and Flynn holed up at third.

Then from five thousand stomping cats there came a crazy sound,
It rocked all through the scene, Man—it really rolled around;
It went right to the top, Dad, and it charged on down below,
For Casey, swinging Casey—he was comin' on to blow!

There was style in Casey's shuffle as he came on with his stick,
There was jive in Casey's strutting, he was on a happy kick;
And when, to clue in all the cats, he doffed his lid real big,
The Square Johns in the group were hip, 'twas Casey on the gig.

Ten thousand peepers piped him as he rubbed fuzz on his palms,
Five thousand choppers grooved it when he smeared some on his arms;
Then while the shook-up pitcher twirled the ball snagged in his clutch,
A hip look lit up Casey, Man, this cat was just too much!

And now the crazy mixed-up ball went flying out through space,
But Casey, he just eyed it with a cool look on his face;
Right at that charged-up sideman, the old ball really sailed,
"That's too far out," sang Casey, "Like, Strike One!" the umpire wailed.

From the pads stacked high with hipsters there was heard a frantic roar,
Like the beating of the bongos from a frenzied Be-Bop score;
"Knife him! Knife that ump, Man!" wailed some weirdo left field clown,
And they would have cut the cat up, but cool Casey put them down.

With a real gone Beatnik grin on him, old Casey cooked with gas,
He fanned down all that ribble, and he sang, "On with this jazz!"
He set the pitcher straight, and once again the old ball flew,
But Casey wouldn't buy it and the ump howled, "Like, Strike Two!"

"He's sick!" wailed all the hipsters, and the Squares, too, sang out "Sick!"
But a nod from Daddy Casey, and those cats got off that kick;
They dug the way he sizzled, like his gaskets were of wax,
They were hip that Casey wouldn't let the ball get by his ax.

The cool look's gone from Casey's chops, his eyes are all popped up,
He stomps his big ax on the plate, he really is hopped up;

And now the pitcher cops the ball, and now it comes on fast,
And now the joint is jumpin' with the sound of Casey's blast.

Man, somewhere in this far-out scene the sun is packing heat,
The group is blowing somewhere and somewhere guts are beat;
And somewhere big cats break up, and small cats raise the roof,
But there is no joy in Endsville—Swinging Casey made a goof.[10]

The lesson of this tribute to De Wolf Hopper seems to be that to succeed in life one should not scruple to build on another's misfortune.

HOPPER AT THE BAT

by William Ludlum—1926

The tale of Casey's fall is meat to every baseball fan,
That tragic tale which Hopper tells as can no other man;
And oft we've thrilled as from his tongue the magic words have flown,
By which we fairly see the game where Mike was overthrown.

Before us Casey swings his bat and pounds the plate; his sneer
Is vividly portrayed to us as he awaits the sphere
In cold contempt to clout it where no fielder ever may
Retrieve that whirling, darting sphere until sometime next day.

We sense the Mudville multitude and all their plaudits meant
To each and every seething soul when Casey's form unbent
In preparation for the swing that never yet had failed,
They knew, with Casey at the bat, they had their pennant nailed!

And there's no doubt it would have been had Casey, as of old,
Accepted opportunity; his fall had ne'er been told
In rhyme for Hopper to recite, and thereby rise to fame—
A thing which never might have been had Casey won that game.

In Casey's failure Hopper saw his chance to please the mob,
And, being such an active guy, he got right on the job;
He's played on our emotions till we've toppled in his hat,
And some believe, instead of Mike, 'twas Hopper at the bat.

The awe of Mudville's thousands is as nothing to compare
With that of all the millions awed when Hopper takes the air;
And though the mighty Casey fanned and failed that ball to kill—
Friend Hopper never has struck out, and likely never will.

If there's a moral to this tale, 'tis all in Casey's stance,
He let the ball go by him twice and, lost his double chance;

But Hopper, with his batting eye, was never much in doubt,
In Casey's failure to connect he saw his chance to clout.

He made a hit and rose to fame on Casey's downward fall—
And every man to win his game must likewise—smite the ball;
'Tis hits that count, and only hits, and when the toss comes true,
Don't let it pass, as Casey did—do as the Hoppers do![11]

Probably the best tribute to the undying fame of Mighty "Casey" was the William Schuman-Jeremy Gury 1953 opera, the subject of the following chapter. Next to that, however, must rank this ballad by the master architect of the "Casey" legend, Grantland Rice. One day in 1926 Rice received the following query: "I have just read your 'Casey's Revenge,' which I understand is a sequel to 'Casey at the Bat.' I had never heard of this poem before. Where can I get a copy?" Rice was so astonished by this question that he used it as the basis for this poem, published in his nationally syndicated column, "The Sportlight," on June 1, 1926.[12]

HE NEVER HEARD OF CASEY

by Grantland Rice—1926

I knew a cove who'd never heard of Washington and Lee,
Of Caesar and Napoleon from the ancient jamboree;
But, bli'me, there are queerer things than anything like that,
For here's a cove who never heard of "Casey at the Bat"!

He never heard of Mudville and its wild and eerie call,
"When Flynn let drive a single to the wonderment of all;"
Nor the stormy roar of welcome that "recoiled upon the flat,
As Casey, Mighty Casey, was advancing to the bat."

"There was ease in Casey's manner," from the Ernest Thayer style,
"There was pride in Casey's bearing," and his tanned face wore a smile;
And when they thundered "Attaboy!" of course he tipped his hat,
But here's a cove who never heard of "Casey at the Bat!"

"Who is Casey?" Can you beat it? Can a thing like this be true?
Is there one who's missed the drama that ripped Mudville through and through?
Is there a fan with soul so dead he never felt the sway,
Of these famous lines by Thayer in the good old Thayer way?

"Ten thousand eyes were on him as he rubbed his hands with dirt,
Five thousand tongues applauded as he wiped them on his shirt;
Then while the writhing pitcher ground the ball into his hip,
Defiance gleamed in Casey's eye, a sneer curled Casey's lip."

The drama grew in force and flame, and berserk went the mob,
With Casey representing more than Hornsby, Ruth, or Cobb;
And as the pitcher cut one loose as if fired from a gat,
Say, here's a guy who never heard of "Casey at the Bat!"

"The sneer is gone from Casey's lip, his teeth are clenched in hate,
He pounds with cruel violence his bat upon the plate";
And as the pitcher shot one through to meet the final test,
There's one low and benighted fan who never heard the rest.

Ten million never heard of Keats, or Shelley, Burns, or Poe,
But they know "the air was shattered by the force of Casey's blow";
They never heard of Shakespeare, nor of Dickens, like as not,
But they know the somber drama from old Mudville's haunted lot.

He never heard of Casey! Am I dreaming? Is it true?
Is fame but wind-blown ashes when the summer day is through?
Does greatness fade so quickly and is grandeur doomed to die,
That bloomed in early morning, ere the dusk rides down the sky.

Is there nothing left immortal in this somber vale called Earth?
Is there nothing that's enduring in its guarding shell of worth?
Is everything forgotten as the new age stumbles on,
And the things that we once cherished make their way to helengon?

Is drifting life but dust and dreams to fade within a flash,
Where one forgets the drama of the Master and the Ash?
Where one has missed the saga with its misty flow of tears,
Upon that day of tragedy beyond the tramping years?

"Oh! Somewhere in this favored land the sun is shining bright,
The band is playing somewhere, and somewhere hearts are light;
And somewhere men are laughing and somewhere children shout,
But there is no joy in Mudville—Mighty Casey has struck out!"

Rise, De Wolf Hopper, in your wrath, and cut the blighter down!
Although Wang may be forgotten in the passing of renown;
There's a graver crime committed which should take you to the mat,
For here's a cove who never heard of "Casey at the Bat!"

I had an epic written which I thought would never die,
Where they'd build a statue for me with its head against the sky;
I said "This will live forever"—but I've canned it in the vat,
For here's a guy who never heard of "Casey at the Bat!" [13]

11.

Grand Opera

The Mighty Casey, a one-act opera, premiered in Hartford, Connecticut, in May 1953. The music was written by the distinguished composer William Schuman, who has always been a baseball enthusiast. As a teenager he aspired to play professional ball. "Baseball was my youth," he writes. "Had I been a better catcher, I might never have become a musician."[1] By his mid-thirties, he was recognized as one of the outstanding composers in the United States. He became president of the Juilliard School of Music in 1935, a post he held until he was named president of New York's Lincoln Center for the Performing Arts in 1962.[2]

Teaming up with Schuman was Jeremy Gury, who wrote the libretto. Like Schuman, Gury is a dyed-in-the-wool baseball fan. A magazine editor and author of children's books, he was, at the time, senior vice-president of the advertising agency Ted Bates and Company, in New York City. Gardner writes that Schuman and Gury "have expanded the Casey myth with such loving insight, such full appreciation of the nuances in Thayer's ballad, that no Casey fan need hesitate to add the opera to the Casey canon. It is sad that Thayer did not live to see it. The details of its plot mesh so smoothly with the poem that one feels at once, 'Yes, of course, that *must* have been the way it happened.' "[3]

Writers had long pondered the unanswered questions posed by "Casey at the Bat." Arthur Robinson, for example, wondered who the opposition and pitcher were, and what "Casey," the man, was like. Naturally, not much could be learned from a baseball poem centering on one half-inning. Consequently, building an opera around a ballad which required less than six minutes to recite demanded much new material. *The Mighty Casey* settled many of the unresolved questions. It put meat on the literary skeleton left by Thayer. Gury even added two new verses, one between the seventh and eighth stanzas, and the other between the eleventh and twelfth stanzas. This was done, he explained, "in order to fill certain dramatic requirements."[4]

The first fact which emerged was that Mudville has a population of 6,732.

Then, at last, we learn what was at stake in the momentous match. It was for the Inter-Urban League title, which meant the state championship. Centerville was the opposing team; its battery was composed of pitcher "Fireball" Snedeker and catcher Thatcher. "Casey's" girl friend, Merry, "is a very attractive typically American girl of about 20," who was active in a local service organization, which within a week or so would be sponsoring a "cake sale" at the Fireman's Carnival. "Mudville Stadium" appeared to be a prosperous operation as it had a watchman, a concessionaire, and several hawkers of peanuts, popcorn, soda, and Cracker Jack in the organization's employment. The watchman was particularly important. He painted the white foul lines and the batter's box and served as narrator of the crucial events which transpired on the field.[5]

The identities of "Casey's" teammates were among the most important new material brought out in *The Mighty Casey*. The chorus introduced each man by position and as his name was called, he stepped forward and recited his skills and qualifications. The pitcher was Andy Jones, a southpaw who had an arsenal of different pitches and was convinced that he was ready for the big leagues. Catcher "Red" O'Toole was a handyman around town, who was batting .372. His son, Mike, will be remembered for his wrong-way run in "O'Toole's Touchdown." First baseman Otis Burrows—librettist Gury, unfortunately, used a corrupted version of "Casey at the Bat"—was chief of the Volunteer Fire Department, and his father operated the local barber shop. Tony Perrone, the second baseman, just loved living in Mudville and managed the Perrone Ice and Coal Company.[6]

Third baseman Elmer Blake moonlighted with his musical combo, the Mudville Melodians. At shortstop, "Scooter" Cooney appeared to be a farm laborer in the employ of "Old Man" Tuthill. They had just laid down thirty-four acres of alfalfa. Not much was revealed about left fielder "Roughhouse" Flynn's off-the-field activities, but on the field he was a tiger. He had been thrown out of eleven games for insulting the umpire and fined seven times. Notwithstanding, he was a valuable man, hitting .328. In center field was popular Benny Rabensky, who liked all the players and all the players liked him. In right field—at last we learn his position—was our hero, "Casey," who was lionized as a wonder, a terror, an idol, a slugger, a king. Despite his impressive statistics— he was batting .564, had knocked in 200 runs, and had belted out 99 home runs—"Mighty Casey" remained mute throughout the entire opera. "We simply felt," the authors wrote, "that one so god-like should not speak. The magnificence of Casey is above mere words."[7]

Two subplots enlivened the story. Centerville's catcher had learned from a spy that "Casey" was a sucker for a high hard one on the inside of the plate, and he discussed the matter at some length with his pitcher Fireball Snedeker. Thatcher would wiggle his ear when he wanted that particular pitch thrown, although it would have made sense to throw that pitch all the time. More serious was Merry's concern over losing her man. The watchman, who seemed to know just about everything, told her that there were two major league scouts in the grandstand—with contracts in their pockets—and if "Casey" had a big day, they would surely sign him and he would leave Mudville for the bright lights of the big city. This unsettled Merry, who sang: "I didn't know this. Casey doesn't want to go. Casey wants to stay here. Oh no! Casey doesn't want to play anywhere but here. Casey doesn't want to leave. It isn't true. There aren't any men. . . . I mean they might have come to watch the others. Casey wouldn't go." The watchman argued that every man should have a chance to make good, but Merry did not want to lose her "Casey."[8]

While the opera filled numerous gaps, it still left one big gap, namely, what happened in the first eight and one-half innings of the game. Scene two commenced with Mudville coming to bat in the last of the ninth, trailing 4–2. Cooney and Burrows were actually put out off stage, but the crowd reaction described their fate. With Mudville down to its last out and Flynn advancing to the bat, Merry prayed that "Casey" would get a chance to bat even though it could mean his departure from town for the majors. But Flynn and Blake got their hits and the crowd went wild. At this point the watchman picked up with the "ease in Casey's manner" and the chorus took over the verse for the next few minutes. Following "a sneer curled Casey's lip," one of the new stanzas was inserted:

The cheering then diminished and the hucksters raucus shout
Was quickly met by threats and cries of "Quiet—throw them out!"
At last the throng fell silent and the barking hawkers quit—
And the only sound was the catcher's hand pounding the catcher's mitt.[9]

After Thatcher and Snedeker refreshed their memories on how to throw to "Casey," the watchman described the first pitch, "strike one!" The crowd was furious, as was the Mudville manager. The latter became so abusive that one is amazed that he was not put out of the game. He practically accused Umpire Buttenheiser of being a "cheat." One had to admire the courage exhibited at this point by Buttenheiser. He fearlessly addressed the crowd in soothing tones, and stated that he was a man of honor and integrity.

I saw the pitch, I made the call,
I called it a strike, you think it's a ball . . .
I call 'em as I see 'em, so if you feel it isn't true . . .
Tell me what, exactly what, precisely what, you're going to do.

He found out what soon enough, as the bottles came raining down on him. Then "Casey" raised his hand and all was still.[10]

The watchman called out the next pitch, "strike two!" which was not followed by the same uproar as strike one, despite the cries of "fraud." After "they knew that Casey wouldn't let that ball go by again," the authors inserted the other new stanza:

> The pitcher moves with caution, his eyes then sweep the field,
> The catcher's hand then gives a sign, the pact between them sealed;
> The pitcher knows his signals, he's been taught by plotting brains,
> A high and inside ball 'twill be, for a single strike remains.

The watchman described the mighty miss as the crowd collapsed back onto the seats, as much from the wind created by "Casey's" swing as from his failure. The chorus handled the last stanza as the spectators sadly made their way homeward.[11]

In the final action of the opera, "Casey" reappeared on the stage and autographed the baseball book of a small boy, to whom he was still a hero despite his strikeout. "Casey" then relived the last pitch, only in this fantasy he connected for a home run and trotted around the bases. Merry appeared and followed him on his imaginary route. "Casey" saw Merry and raced to her. They embraced and walked off the stage hand in hand; he would not be leaving Mudville after all.[12]

To date *The Mighty Casey* has not exactly been a scintillating success. Not that every masterpiece in the archives of opera has always been recognized as such at the outset. The CBS television program "Omnibus" carried the eighty-minute work on March 6, 1955, while small companies in several cities have also presented it. Appropriately, one of these was Stockton, California. On more than one occasion it has been produced in Japan, and that is about it.[13] That it will ever become part of the standard repertoire of the Metropolitan, Covent Garden, or La Scala is most unlikely.

12.

Mighty Casey: All-American

To explain the timeless appeal of "Casey at the Bat" one must consider the role of baseball in American culture and society. The game has been so much a part of our national life for nearly a century and a half that it is unnecessary to prove the point. Grown men play it, scholars write about it, and presidents pay homage to it. Its language, its legends, and its heroes have become part of the American heritage. Whether as a multimillion dollar business or as child's play, its influence has been unmistakable. Jacques Barzun, French-born cultural historian, cogently made the point: "Whoever wants to know the heart and mind of America had better learn baseball, the rules and realities of the game."[1]

Sportswriters have always assumed the importance of the National Pastime, but recognition from the intellectual community that baseball has been a vital force in our country's history and a mirror of social change has been slow to develop. Yet Bruce Catton, Civil War historian, has said, "Baseball is the American game, great or otherwise, because it reflects so perfectly certain aspects of the American character that no other sport quite portrays."[2] Other historians, sociologists, and literary critics are now confirming this "truth." It is not a proposition subject to scientific verification. Rather, the evidence is impressionistic, "experiential," drawn from the memories of four generations of baseball fans.

What has been baseball's appeal? A search of the works of writers and historians reveals a common ground of opinion. The grandeur of an afternoon in the sun (night baseball, of course, destroyed this), the excitement, the developing drama as a close game unfolds, the ecstatic joy at victory, the uncontrollable gloom at defeat. Watching the great stars of the day, whether they be Hamilton, Delahanty, and Young, or Ruth, Cobb, and Speaker, or Musial, Williams, and DiMaggio, or Rose, Yastrzemski, and Carlton. Seeing the spectacular play—the unassisted "twin-killing," the steal of home, or the "grand slam." Anticipating the three-and-two pitch, especially in the bottom of the ninth inning with the score tied, the bases loaded and two men out. Personally, in the hundreds of games I have seen something unexpected or incredible seemed to happen in almost every one.

In 1911 William Patten and J. Walker McSpadden wrote that baseball was "an ideal sport—strong, manly, clean—furnishing equal interest to both participant and spectators—it has waxed mightier and mightier until it is indeed the National Game, and perhaps the greatest national game that any country ever saw." H. Addington Bruce agreed. In 1913 he observed that "Veritably baseball is something more than the great American game—it is an American institution having a significant place in the life of the people. . . . " To illustrate his point he reported that the members of the United States Supreme Court were so eager to know the progress of play in the 1912 World Series that they received inning-by-inning reports while on the bench listening to arguments in the "bath-tub trust" case.[3]

The following year Francis Richter wrote that "Baseball is a game that lends itself readily to sentiment, emotion, enthusiasm and idealism; because being typical of a race, it responds to all of the mental attributes and the characteristics of that race; and therefore it is capable of appeal through the mind and heart as well as through the senses." In a letter to Arthur Mann, novelist Thomas Wolfe wrote shortly before his death in 1938, "One reason I have always loved baseball so much is that it has been not merely "the national game" but really a part of . . . the million memories of America."[4]

Lee Allen in 1951 observed that "fans look for and receive everything from baseball: thrills that border on ecstasy, intense excitement, and inevitably, glum disappointment. But seldom are they bored, and through the winters that interrupt their passion they remember all the victories and even the lost causes of the deep purple past with sweet nostalgia that will never be forgotten."[5] Roger Angell touched upon a somewhat similar theme when he spoke of the "inner game," or "baseball in the mind." "There is no fan who does not know it. It is a game of recollections, recapturings, and visions; figures and occasions return. . . . By thinking about baseball like this, by playing it over and yet keeping it to ourselves we begin to make discoveries. With luck, we may even penetrate some of its mysteries and learn once again how richly and variously the game can reward us." No other sport, Angell added, can provide this experience, "these permanent interior pictures, these ancient and precise excitements."[6]

Moreover, it is a sport that over the years has changed only in small ways. A refugee from the 1860s planted in our midst today would easily recognize the game he knew. He might be puzzled by some of the rules changes and curious about the designated hitter, but he would quickly catch on. That is why, in the "Author's Note" to their opera "The Mighty Casey," William Schuman and Jeremy Gury emphasized that the time setting is "not so long ago." Baseball—and "Casey"—should be enjoyed by Americans of any generation. Bruce Catton wrote that baseball is "an unchanging pageant . . . and although it is wholly urbanized it still speaks of the small town and the simple, rural era that lived before the automobile came in to blight the landscape."[7]

How does one become addicted to this National Pastime which, as so many have testified, became a part of the warp and the woof of the American social fabric? Again, this is not easy to put into words. "I wish," wrote Art Hill, "I could explain my lifelong obsession with baseball. But that is like trying to explain sex to a precocious six-year-old. . . . I know only that I became a lifelong Detroit Tiger fan the day I saw my first major league game at the age of nine." [8]

My own experience was somewhat similar. Having two older brothers who spoke of Ruth, Speaker, Paul Waner, and others much of the time, I was curious as to who and what they were talking about. At length, an indulgent father took me to Cleveland's old League Park on Saturday, August 10, 1929—that's the kind of impression the first game made upon me. Coming up the ramp, the instant panorama of glowing green turf, the white foul lines, the rich earthen infield, and the magnificent double-decked grandstands (which sat only 24,000 people, but they were grander than anything in my brief experience), struck with the force of a Niagara or a Grand Canyon. I was an easy mark before the first ball was pitched. And the Yankees were in town with Ruth and Gehrig. The Babe promptly obliged me with his 499th career home run over the right field fence onto Lexington Avenue. With my curiosity only partly assuaged and my interest quickened, I bought my first baseball book—the 1929 *Who's Who in Baseball*. I have been buying baseball books ever since.

But Art Hill and I were only two among millions of Americans who became "hooked" on baseball in their early years. Douglass Wallop captured the idea when he wrote, "Only yesterday the fan [of today] was a kid of nine or ten bolting his breakfast on Saturday morning and hurtling from the house with a glove buttoned over his belt and a bat over his shoulder, rushing to the nearest vacant lot . . . where the other guys were gathering, a place where it would always be spring. For him, baseball would always have the sound and smell of that morning." [9]

There were occasional exceptions to this rule; writer James Farrell's grandmother was one. She migrated to the United States from Ireland during the Civil War and settled in Brooklyn. Later she moved to Chicago. Her grandson wrote that she never quite understood all the change that was taking place in her adopted country, but one institution she fell in love with was baseball. "Once she saw a game she wanted to see more, and as a little old woman, in her Sunday dress, she went to ladies day games alone in the early 1920's. Not telling anyone where she was going, she would dress up of a Friday afternoon and go to Comiskey Park on the street car. She came home excited. . . . Baseball to her was part of the new world of America, but she saw it with the wonder of an unlettered peasant woman." [10]

Speaking of the 1929 *Who's Who in Baseball* brings up one of baseball's most intriguing attributes—statistics. No sport approaches baseball in its records and record-keeping. Of course, the game has the longest history of any major team sport, which explains the bulky encyclopedias, but apart from that it is admirably designed for numerical compilations and calculations. One of the fun aspects is checking over the weekly and annual batting averages and pitching percentages. The assault on long-standing records has become a national event: Roger Maris's 61st home run, Hank Aaron's 715th home run, Pete Rose's 44 game hitting streak and his 4,000th base hit as he closed in on Ty Cobb's 4,191 mark. The breaking of Ty Cobb's base-stealing record by Maury Wills, then by Lou Brock, and then by Ricky Henderson, excited new interest in what had become a lost art.

The special vocabulary of baseball, or "cant" as Tristram Coffin called it, is far greater than that of any other sport. Not only is it great in volume, the sheer amount of "baseballese" which has worked its way into standard English is even more impressive. "No other sport," wrote Coffin, "has contributed even a fraction of the phrases and words baseball has. There is some truth in the statement that a foreigner wishing to learn our language might as well start at the ballpark." He listed nearly a column of words, terms, and phrases drawn from the game to illustrate the point. Summing up, Coffin suggested that the claims of other sports that they are supplanting baseball as our national game may have "two strikes" on them when they "come to bat." [11]

Moreover, baseball has by far the largest library of literature of any sport. Its long history again explains part of this, but the game itself is the major reason. Being an important part of American life, it is worth writing about. In his 1975 Guide to Baseball Literature, Anton Grobani listed over 3,000 publications in thirty-three categories. Works of nonfiction numbered about 750, while those of fiction, humor, and verse about 625. As early as 1914 Richter wrote that baseball had "not only created a literature of its own, but it has inspired the poets, romancers and wits of two generations to literary efforts of many kinds and various degrees of order." [12]

The not inconsiderable impact of baseball on American fiction has been traced by Ralph S. Graber. The early writings about Frank Merriwell, Lefty Locke, and Baseball Joe were geared to the juvenile market and were marred by "stock characterization, stilted dialogue, improbable situations, and heavy moralizing." While boys loved them—judging by the volume of sales—these works hardly rated as important literature. Beginning in the 1920s, however, not only did the quality of baseball fiction improve, it was now directed more at adult audiences. Such writers as Heywood Broun and Ring Lardner were far more realistic in their short stories and books and dealt with themes which, transcending the limits of bseball, examined the human condition. [13]

The upward trend continued in the 1930s and 1940s, with writers like Thomas Wolfe and James Farrell utilizing baseball situations to probe life's complex problems. Nelson Algren, Robert Penn Warren, and James Thurber also wrote solid baseball stories or worked baseball into their central themes. Juveniles were not neglected either, but the output here was far more sophisticated than the stereotyped writings of the pre-World War I era. Since World War II baseball fiction has followed two paths—farce and fantasy, and down-to-earth realism. The novels of Eliot Asinof, Bernard Malamud, and Mark Harris fall into the latter category. Obviously, the interest of writers in baseball and in relating it to society at large shows no sign of abating.[14]

In speaking of the literature of the National Pastime, one of the game's Founding Fathers, Albert G. Spalding, observed that "Love has its sonnets galore; war has its epics in heroic verse; tragedy its sombre story in measured lines and baseball has its 'Casey at the Bat.' " Although the poem may not be as well known today as it was to earlier generations, it still ranks as the most celebrated poem in all of American sport. It is the classic of the national game. Not every human emotion is found in those thirteen stanzas, but many of them are. Imminent defeat, restored hope, expectant triumph, and then crushing tragedy. Historian Earl Schenk Miers remembered how we exulted to "Take Me Out to the Ball Game," and also—speaking of "Casey"—how we suffered "in our hearts for that fallen hero."[15]

"Casey at the Bat" is approaching its centennial. It has enjoyed this near century of acclaim because it seemed to touch something central in the American spirit. It happened to talk about baseball, but the theme transcended the National Pastime and spoke of human success and failure in a larger setting.

Those who heard De Wolf Hopper must have enjoyed a great experience, although not necessarily a unique one. He recited "Casey" over ten thousand times, and if only a hundred people heard him each time, the minimum number would have been one million. It is likely that many millions heard him since the performance was one of the most celebrated events in theatrical circles in the first third of the twentieth century. Hopper was gone by my time, but the impact he made had already penetrated the sacred precincts of academe. One of my early exposures to the "classic" was as an undergraduate at Wooster College in 1941. During a (compulsory) chapel service the college president, Dr. Charles F. Wishart, recited "Casey at the Bat." "Prexy" was in his sixties, had a massive mane of white hair, and represented the scholar exemplar of that age. To listen to this distinguished theologian deliver those hallowed lines, during a chapel service of all places, convinced me the poem possessed eternal qualities.[16]

Probably no records exist on the subject, but "Casey at the Bat" has to be one of the most parodied poems in literary annals. Seventy-five or so have been reprinted in this volume, and one can be certain that this collection is not exhaustive. In itself this is a remarkable tribute. As a regular reader of old *Sporting Lifes*, *The Sporting Newses*, and *Baseball Magazines*, I have become accustomed to encountering "Casey" poems at regular intervals. They usually dealt with baseball, but occasionally other sports. One can almost trace the rise of the National Pastime and its heroes by the subject matter of the "Casey Canon" over the years.

No one will argue that all of this is great literature. The basic verses by Thayer and Rice were imaginative and clever, but most of what followed was sophomoric doggerel. The meter was frequently "out of sync," the English language was brutalized, and the happenings were preposterous. Casey achieved, or failed to achieve, many outlandish goals and did many ridiculous things. But because his "greatness" had been established early, these later absurdities were happily tolerated.

That the verses are not great in themselves, however, is unimportant because they have become part of the legend, the myth, the canon that has preserved "Casey's" name for four generations. Knowing what happened on that famous day in Mudville, the informed ones are prepared for each new verse—and absurdity—that appears, prepared to either accommodate it in the frame already constructed or expose it as a wild aberration. Either way it becomes an addition to the developing lore. It would have been nice if all "Casey" poems had proceeded as logical extensions of the original, but that was not to be. And perhaps some of the charm of the canon is its absence of rationality. One could never be sure what "Casey" (or those who shone in his reflected fame) was up to.

Following the Hartford premiere of *The Mighty Casey* in 1953, Harold C. Schonberg, music critic for the *New York Times*, noted that the music was lively and amusing and quite suited to Thayer's "pleasant little fable." This aroused the hackles of the guardian of the "Casey" canon. "Can it be," Gardner demanded to know, "that the music critic of the *New York Times* is not a baseball fan? Pleasant little fable, indeed! *Casey* is neither pleasant nor little. It is tragic and titanic." [17]

Was, is, "Casey at the Bat" titanic or merely trivial? Academic people seem to disagree on the subject. Folklorist and critic Tristram Coffin, in analyzing the sports fiction of "Never-Never Land"—works which glorified the feats of the Frank Merriwells, the Baseball Joes, and the Dink Stovers—concluded that it was all pretty poor. The Stover stories by Owen Johnson were the "best," but that tribute had to be quickly qualified by the phrase "of a bad lot." Coffin next turned to "Casey." "Surely without a 'bad lot' . . . framing it 'Casey at the Bat' could never have scored its steady success. For the defeated Casey, not the triumphant pitcher, is the hero of the wistful poem. There is refreshment in hearing that 'there is no joy in Mudville' and that at least one of these Merriwells of a thousand 'hot finishes' has actually struck out." So "Casey" is better than most of the "Never-Never Land" writing, concluded Coffin, but it is still trash; it "went out of most homes with the garbage," and was only rescued from oblivion by chance. [18]

On the other hand, literary critic William Lyon Phelps of Yale in 1934 submitted that Ernest L. Thayer had written "a masterpiece which millions of ambitious men wish they had written, for *Casey* is absolute perfection. The psychology of the hero and the psychology of the crowd leave nothing to be desired. There is more knowledge of human nature displayed in this poem than in many of the works of the psychiatrist." [19] Howard Lowry, future president of Wooster, who had urged "Prexy" Wishart to recite "Casey" in chapel, was a lit-

erary scholar himself, and he believed that the poem was "an important con-
tribution to American folklore."[20]

Unconcerned over either its titanic or its trashy qualities, the general public
has already enjoyed "Casey at the Bat" for a century and may continue to enjoy it for another one hundred years.

Chronology

The main events in the "Casey chronology," except for the publication dates for the poems, are listed below in order. The births and deaths of the major characters, release dates of important books, and stages in the principal controversies are included in this material.

1859 Birth of "Mighty Casey"
1863 Birth of Ernest L. Thayer
1865 Birth of Dan Casey
1876 Will Valentine arrives in the United States
1882
or
1886 Frank J. Wilstach asserts that Valentine wrote "Casey at the Bat" as a parody on Thomas Macaulay's "Horatius at the Bridge"
1885 Thayer graduates from Harvard
     George Whitefield D'Vys claims he wrote "Casey at the Bat"—eight stanzas only—at this time
1886 D'Vys claims that his "Casey at the Bat" was published in the *Sporting Times* at this time
     Mike "King" Kelly sold from Chicago to Boston for the unheard-of price of $10,000
     Thayer joins the staff of the *San Francisco Examiner*
1887 Dan Casey claims that the game in which he struck out and upon which Thayer based "Casey at the Bat" occurred at this time
1888 "Casey at the Bat" published in *San Francisco Examiner*
     Shortened version of "Casey at the Bat" with "Kelly" substituted for "Casey" published in *Sporting Times*
1889 De Wolf Hopper recites "Casey at the Bat" for first time in Wallack's Theater in New York City
1892
or
1893 Hopper begins regular recitations of "Casey at the Bat"
     Hopper meets Thayer
1894 "King" Kelly dies

1896   Thayer writes comic ballads for *New York Journal*
1897   D'Vys loses his only copy of 1886 *Sporting Times*, which he claimed carried his
          eight-stanza "Casey at the Bat"
1900   Dan Casey injured in trolley accident in Binghamton, New York
1901   John Patrick Parnell Cahill, who claimed to be the prototype for Thayer's "Casey,"
          dies
1902   Frederic L. Knowles's anthology, *A Treasury of Humorous Poetry*, which in-
          cluded "Casey at the Bat," is published
1905   Editorial in *The Sporting News* debates issue of authorship of "Casey at the Bat"
          Louisville writer Lee Goldberg contends that Valentine wrote "Casey at the Bat"
1906   Baltimore writer Joseph Cummings argues that Thayer wrote "Casey at the Bat"
          Grantland Rice writes "Casey's Revenge"
1908   John Glenister writes article, "Who Wrote 'Casey at the Bat'?"
          Homer Croy writes article, "Casey at the Bat"
          Harry Thurston Peck publishes his findings on authorship issue, "Who Wrote
          'Casey at the Bat'?"
1909   Dennis Casey, brother of Dan, dies
1910   Rice publishes anthology of his verses, *Baseball Ballads*
1911   Albert G. Spalding publishes his *America's National Game*
          Alfred Spink publishes the second edition of his *The National Game*
1912   Thayer settles in Santa Barbara, California
1913   Thayer marries Rosalind Burl Hammett, a widow
1914   Francis Richter publishes his *History and Records of Baseball*
1916   Silent movie, "Casey at the Bat," starring De Wolf Hopper, is released
1923   Burton E. Stevenson publishes first edition of his *Famous Single Poems*
          A number of articles are published in *The Sporting News* debating the issues of
          authorship and if there was a real "Casey"
1925   First printing of Hopper's autobiography, *Once a Clown Always a Clown*, is re-
          leased. Other printings occurred in 1926 and 1927
1927   Silent movie, "Casey at the Bat," starring Wallace Beery, is released
1932   D'Vys again claims he wrote "Casey at the Bat." Thayer again denies the claim
1934   William Lyon Phelps publishes *What I Like in Poetry*
1935   Second edition of Stevenson's *Famous Single Poems* is published
          Dan Casey claims again—he has made the claim before but no dates for earlier
          claims can be found—that he was the original "Casey" and that "the game"
          took place in 1887 in Philadelphia
1936   O. Robinson Casey, who also claimed to be the original "Casey," dies
          Hazel Felleman's *Best Loved Poems* is published
1938   Dan Casey, on Gabriel Heatter's radio program, insists again that he was the real
          "Casey" which revives the controversy and prompts a series of articles and
          letters in *The Sporting News* for the next few weeks
1940   Thayer dies
1941   D'Vys dies
          Rice publishes his second anthology of verses, *Only the Brave*
1943   Dan Casey dies
1946   "Mighty Casey" dies, according to Martin Gardner
          "Casey at the Bat" is produced in an animated cartoon by Walt Disney Produc-
          tions with actor Jerry Colonna reciting the poem

1952–

1955   Reenactments of "Casey at the Bat" take place in Stockton, California, which, according to some, was the original "Mudville"

1953   A second animated cartoon, "Casey at the Bat," is released by Walt Disney Productions

William Schuman-Jeremy Gury opera, *The Mighty Casey*, premieres in Hartford, Connecticut

1954   Arthur L. Bloomfield writes a short essay, "Horatius at the Bridge and Casey at the Bat," in which he argues that "Casey at the Bat" is a parody of Macaulay's "Horatius at the Bridge"

Darrell Berrigan writes article "The Truth About Casey" in the *Saturday Evening Post*

Charles O. Kennedy publishes *A Treasury of American Ballads: Gay, Naughty, and Classic*, in which he argues that Thayer wrote "Casey's Revenge"

1955   Lee Allen publishes *Hot Stove League* with a chapter on "Casey at the Bat"

1956   *Sports Illustrated* publishes a cartoon drawing of "Casey at the Bat"

1959   Richard Dunlop writes article "Was This the Real Casey?" in *Baseball Digest*

1960   Joanne Mary Ghio writes article "Stockton is Casey's Mudville" in *Baseball Digest*

1962   Leonard Koppett writes article "The Day 'Casey' First Appeared" in *Baseball Digest*

1963   Anthony Austin writes article "75 years Later" in *New York Times Magazine*

1964   Franklin Watts and Prentice-Hall publish illustrated hard-bound editions of "Casey at the Bat"

1967   Martin Gardner publishes *The Annotated Casey at the Bat*

1971   Third edition of Stevenson's *Famous Single Poems* is published

1972   Foster Brooks, "Casey" authority, appears on Joe Garagiola show

1975   Tristram Coffin publishes *The Illustrated Book of Baseball Folklore*

Notes

Chapter 1: The Debut

1. *San Francisco Examiner*, June 3, 1888.

2. Martin Gardner, *The Annotated Casey at the Bat* (New York: Clarkson N. Potter, Inc., 1967), pp. 199–206.

3. The date has been in dispute. Hopper in his memoirs said the day of his first recital of "Casey" was May 13, 1888, an obvious error since the poem had not yet been published. It was assumed that he meant May 13, 1889, but a check of the records revealed that on that day Cleveland, not Chicago, was playing in New York. In a later letter to Burton E. Stevenson, Hopper conceded that the time was probably August 1888. This is now assumed to be the correct month, though the date itself has not been established. De Wolf Hopper with Wesley Winans Stout, *Reminiscences of De Wolf Hopper: Once a Clown Always a Clown* (Garden City, N.Y.: Garden City Publishing Co., 1925), p. 72; *The Sporting News*, March 31, 1938 (hereafter cited as *SN*); Burton E. Stevenson, *Famous Single Poems* (Freeport, N.Y.: Books for Libraries Press, 1971), p. 125; Gardner, *Annotated Casey*, p. 175.

4. Hopper, *Always a Clown*, pp. 77–78.

5. Ibid., pp. 80 -81.

6. Ibid., pp. 72–73.

7. Ibid., pp. 84–85; Anthony Austin, "Seventy-Five Years Ago," *New York Times Magazine*, June 9, 1963, pp. 51, 54. While Hopper immortalized "Casey," Pat White, a burlesque comic, is supposed to have been the first actor to dramatize the poem on stage. White had played amateur ball in Michigan and incorporated some of those experiences into a one-act skit, "Doings in Mudville," an enlarged rendition of "Casey at the Bat." *Cleveland Leader*, March 14, 1909.

8. Frederic Lawrence Knowles, *A Treasury of Humorous Poetry* (Boston: Dana, Estes and Co., Publishers, 1902), pp. 297–99; reprinted in Gardner, *Annotated Casey*, pp. 27–29.

Chapter 2: Search for the Author

1. Hopper, *Always a Clown*, p. 85.

2. Ibid., pp. 86–87.

3. Stevenson, *Famous Single Poems*, pp. 110–11; Gardner, *Annotated Casey*, p. 26.

4. *SN*, January 28, 1905; Stevenson, *Famous Single Poems*, p. 113. In other places Wilstach stated the year of publication to be 1886. Harry Thurston Peck, "Who Wrote 'Casey at the Bat'?" *The Scrap Book* 6 (December 1908): 950.

5. *SN*, January 28, 1905.

6. Ibid., January 20, 1906.

7. Ibid. Albert G. Spalding found the clipping containing this letter among Henry "Father" Chadwick's papers which had been given him by Chadwick's widow, and published it, with a few minor errors, in his *America's National Game* (New York: American Sports Publishing Co., 1911), p. 452.

8. *SN*, January 20, 1906.

9. Lee Allen, *The Hot Stove League* (New York: A. S. Barnes and Co., 1955), p. 197.

10. Homer Croy, "Casey at the Bat," *Baseball Magazine*, October 1908, p. 10.

11. John W. Glenister, "Who Wrote 'Casey at the Bat'?" *Baseball Magazine*, June 1908, p. 60.

12. Peck, "Who Wrote 'Casey at the Bat'?" p. 947.

13. Ibid., p. 949.

14. Ibid., pp. 949–50.

15. Ibid., p. 950.

16. On September 16, 1908, three months before the *Scrap Book* article appeared, Peck wrote to Harry K. Williams, another of Thayer's classmates: "In reply to your letter of the 15th inst., I would say that the evidence with regard to 'Casey at the Bat' seems to my mind to be complete; and I may inform you in confidence that Mr. Thayer's claim to its authorship cannot seriously be questioned. The article on the subject, with a synopsis of the evidence, will appear in *The Scrap Book* for December." *SN*, April 7, 1938.

17. Peck, "Who Wrote 'Casey at the Bat'?" p. 950.

18. Ibid.

19. Ibid., pp. 950–51.

20. Ibid., p. 951.

21. Ibid., pp. 951–52.

22. Ibid.

23. Ibid., p. 952.

24. Ibid., pp. 952–53.

25. Ibid., p. 953. It is surprising that Kelly was D'Vys's hero in 1885 since Boston did not acquire him from Chicago until after the 1886 season.

26. Ibid.

27. Ibid., pp. 953–54.

28. Ibid., p. 954.

29. Gardner, *Annotated Casey*, p. 175; Stevenson, *Famous Single Poems*.

30. Stevenson, *Famous Single Poems*, pp. 110–11; Francis C. Richter, *History and Records of Baseball* (Philadelphia: published by author, 1914), pp. 299–306. Harry Clay Palmer, *Athletic Sports in America, England, and Australia* (Philadelphia: Hubbard

Brothers, Publishers, 1889), pp. 575–610, has an extensive section on sportswriters of the 1880s with sketches and pictures, but there is no Joseph Quinlan Murphy among them.

31. Stevenson, *Famous Single Poems*, pp. 111–13.

32. Ibid. It should be noted that in Wilstach's earlier claim, cited in Goldberg's column, Valentine wrote the poem in 1882, rather than in 1886, which if true would have left the question still open in spite of this search of the *Tribune* files.

33. Stevenson, *Famous Single Poems*, pp. 116–17.

34. Ibid., pp. 118–19.

35. Ibid., p. 123.

36. *New York Times*, March 13, 1932.

37. *SN*, March 10, 31, April 7, May 12, 1938.

38. Ibid., August 29, 1940, June 5, 1941. After leaving the family business in the 1890s Thayer traveled extensively abroad and settled down in Santa Barbara in 1912, where he lived his remaining years. He married a widow, Rosalind Burl Hammett, in 1913, who survived him. She had two sons by her first husband, but she and Thayer had no children. Never pressed for money, Thayer spent his later years "in philosophical study and in writing, but not for publication." Friends urged him to write, but he would always decline, observing "I have nothing to say." He changed his mind toward the end of his life, but time had run out on him. "Now I have something to say," he commented, "and I am too weak to say it." *National Cyclopedia of American Biography* XXXIII (New York, 1947): 104–5; Gardner, *Annotated Casey*, p. 16.

39. Gardner, *Annotated Casey*, p. 32; Stevenson, *Famous Single Poems*, p. 126.

40. Gardner, *Annotated Casey*, pp. 33–35.

Chapter 3: Who Was "Casey"?

1. *SN*, November 15, 1923.

2. Ibid., November 15, 29, 1923; *Baseball Encyclopedia* (New York: Macmillan, 1974), p. 326.

3. Joanne Mary Ghio, "Stockton is Casey's Mudville," *Baseball Digest*, May 1960, p. 93.

4. *SN*, November 9, 1901.

5. Spalding, *America's National Game*, p. 453.

6. *SN*, November 29, 1923.

7. Ibid., November 9, 1901.

8. *Baseball Encyclopedia*, p. 986; *SN*, February 18, 1943. In a 1935 interview with *The Sporting News*, Dan Casey said that Ernest Thayer was a Philadelphia sportswriter in 1887 who had covered the game in which he struck out. He said that Thayer wrote "Casey at the Bat" following the game. *SN*, May 23, 1935.

9. *SN*, November 15, 1923.

10. Ibid., May 23, 1935, February 18, 1943.

11. Ibid., March 10, 1938, February 18, 1943. In Richard Dunlop, "Was This the Real Casey?" *Baseball Digest*, July 1959, pp. 41–42, Casey gave essentially the same story.

12. *SN*, February 18, 1943.

13. Ibid.

14. Ibid., March 17, 1938. Goodfriend's contention prompted veteran baseball writer Guy McQ. Smith to wonder "what the heck was King Kelly doing at Wallack's that

night, when at the time he was a member of the Boston'' team, which was playing somewhere else. Ibid.

15. Ibid.; Dunlop, "Was This the Real Casey?" p. 42.

16. *SN*, February 18, 1943.

17. Ibid., November 15, 1923; Allen, *Hot Stove League*, p. 200; *Baseball Encyclopedia*, p. 336.

18. Allen, *Hot Stove League*, p. 211.

19. *Spalding Baseball Guide*, 1884 Edition, pp. 66–68.

20. James Bready, *The Home Team* (Washington, D.C.: published by author, 1971), p. 15.

21. Ibid.

22. Ibid.

23. Ibid.

24. *Baseball Encyclopedia*, p. 560; Gardner, *Annotated Casey*, pp. 183–84.

25. *Baseball Encyclopedia*, p. 560; Gardner, *Annotated Casey*, p. 184.

26. Gardner, *Annotated Casey*, pp. 185–86.

27. *SN*, March 31, 1938.

28. Charles O'Brien Kennedy, *A Treasury of American Ballads, Gay, Naughty, and Classic* (New York: The McBride Co., 1954), p. 222.

29. *SN*, March 31, 1938.

30. Croy, "Casey at the Bat," p. 11.

31. A multicolored copy of this painting accompanied Darrell Berrigan's "The Truth About Casey," *Saturday Evening Post*, July 3, 1954, p. 30. Gardner included a black and white copy on page 17 of his *Annotated Casey*.

32. Gardner included this picture on page 23 of his *Annotated Casey*.

33. *Casey at the Bat*, illustrated by Paul Frame (Englewood Cliffs: Prentice-Hall, 1964).

34. *Stockton* (Calif.) *Record*, June 12, 1953; *SN*, May 12, 1948, April 12, 1950; *Pittsburgh Press*, April 11, 1976.

35. *Saturday Evening Post*, Summer 1972, p. 87; Gardner, *Annotated Casey*, p. 11; *Sports Illustrated*, April 9, 1956, pp. 47–50; *Casey at the Bat*, illustrated by Jim Hull (New York: Dover Publications, 1977).

36. *Casey at the Bat* (New York: New Amsterdam Book Co., 1901; reprinted by Castle Press, Pasadena, Calif., 1977).

37. Berrigan, "The Truth About Casey," p. 94.

Chapter 4: Where Was Mudville?

1. *Stockton Record*, August 27, 29, 30, 1952.

2. Ibid.

3. Ibid., June 12, 1953.

4. Ibid. Following the second reenactment, the Stockton Chamber of Commerce proposed the creation of a "Casey Award," to be given annually to the major league player with the fewest strikeouts. *SN*, September 2, 1953.

5. *Stockton Record*, June 3, 5, 1954.

6. Ibid.

7. This was the article written by Darrell Berrigan, "The Truth About Casey."

8. *Stockton Record*, June 3, 5, 1954.

9. Ibid., June 7, 1954.

10. Ibid., June 11, 1955.

11. Ibid.

12. Isabel M. Benson to author, July 21, 1972.

13. Berrigan, "The Truth About Casey," p. 30.

14. Ibid., pp. 30, 94.

15. Ibid., pp. 30, 92, 94.

16. Ibid., p. 30. Quite recently the Stockton claim has been revived. In 1983 the Stockton club of the California League was nicknamed the "Mudville Ports," and the club's uniform carried the name "Mudville," not "Stockton," on the shirt front. *Lake County* (Ohio) *News-Herald*, May 29, 1983.

17. Ibid.

18. Ghio, "Stockton is Casey's Mudville," p. 93; Berrigan, "The Truth About Casey," pp. 93–94; Spalding, *America's National Game*, pp. 251–65. Harry Clay Palmer devoted nearly one-half of his massive *Athletic Sports in America, England, and Australia* to the world tour.

19. *Stockton Record*, August 27, 1952, June 12, 1953.

20. Ghio, "Stockton is Casey's Mudville," pp. 93–94; Gardner to author, July 13, 1972.

21. Ghio, "Stockton is Casey's Mudville," pp. 93–94.

22. Ibid., p. 94.

23. Wesley Simard, an unreconstructed Stocktonian, was positive his home town was the place. He wrote that "Thayer's masterpiece was written about our own Stockton baseball team," and again, "Documented evidence has been found proving that Stockton was the unfortunate Mudville team," and still again, "Stockton is generally conceded by even the most cynical as the home of 'Casey at the Bat'." Simard, "Casey at the Bat," *Far Westerner*, July 1966, p. 8.

24. Centerville was Mudville's opponent on that unforgettable day.

25. Gardner, *Annotated Casey*, p. 177.

26. Ibid., pp. 188, 190, 192.

Chapter 5: The Pitcher

1. Gardner, *Annotated Casey*, p. 122.

2. Ibid., pp. 88, 176.

3. Ibid., pp. 89–90.

4. *SN*, February 5, 1925.

5. Gardner, *Annotated Casey*, pp. 123–24.

6. This verse was recited by Foster Brooks at a breakfast interview and was reprinted in the *Pittsburgh Press*, June 18, 1972.

7. *SN*, June 10, 1937. Don Fairbairn was identified as the "poet laureate" of the *Philadelphia Evening Bulletin*. In a study of superstitions in a Kentucky county, a writer mentions one with baseball applications. "If a baseball player sees a cross-eyed woman in the grandstand, he will not get a hit during the game." As folklorist Tristram P. Coffin points out, however, "cross-eyed women are bad luck in all British-derived cultures." Coffin, *The Illustrated Book of Baseball Folklore* (New York: The Seabury Press, 1975), pp. 38–39. This book was originally published as *The Old Ball Game: Baseball in Folklore and Fiction* (New York: Herder and Herder, 1971).

8. This verse accompanied an Adirondack bat advertisement, *SN*, May 12, 1948.

9. Leonard Koppett, "The Day 'Casey' First Appeared," *Baseball Digest*, February 1962, pp. 20–22.

10. Arthur Robinson, "Casey's Daughter at the Bat," Charles Einstein, ed., *The Third Fireside Book of Baseball* (New York: Simon and Schuster, 1968), p. 390.

Chapter 6: Redemption

1. *SN*, November 11, 1899.

2. *Sporting Life*, April 22, 1905 (hereafter cited as *SL*), reprinted from *San Francisco Examiner*.

3. *The Speaker* 2 (June 1907): 205–7; Gardner, *Annotated Casey*, p. 38.

4. Hazel Felleman, *Best Loved Poems of the American People* (Garden City, N.Y.: Doubleday and Co., 1936), pp. 284–85; Gardner, *Annotated Casey*, p. 38.

5. *Stockton Record*, December 30, 1952; *New York Times*, September 9, 14, 1958; Kennedy, *A Treasury of American Ballads*, pp. 225–28; Coffin, *Illustrated Book of Baseball Folklore*, p. 133. Joanne Mary Ghio also believed that Thayer wrote both poems. "Stockton is Casey's Mudville," p. 93. Coffin, however, was primarily concerned with the quality of the poetry, not the question of authorship. *Illustrated Book of Baseball Folklore*, p. 133 (note); Coffin to author, March 22, 1983.

6. Grantland Rice, *Baseball Ballads* (Nashville: The Tennesseean Company, 1910); Grantland Rice, *Only the Brave* (New York: A. S. Barnes and Co., 1941); Dave Camerer, ed., *The Best of Grantland Rice* (New York: Franklin Watts, Inc., 1963); Grantland Rice, *The Tumult and the Shouting* (New York: A. S. Barnes and Co., 1954); *SL*, November 24, 1906.

7. Gardner, *Annotated Casey*, pp. 39–41.

8. Grantland Rice, *Only the Brave*, pp. 125–29.

9. "The Windup," (published by Stan W. Carlson, Minneapolis, Minn., 1939), p. 62.

10. *San Francisco Examiner*, July 26, 1908.

11. *SL*, December 12, 1912. In stanza six, line one, "woobly" is correct. In stanza six, line three, "as the most big leaguers do" is correct. It should be noted that "Casey" had learned to hit the spitball.

12. *Baseball Magazine*, September 1914, pp. 79–80.

13. Ibid., June 1922, p. 319. Gardner explained the significance of the "goat gland" in the last line. "At the time," he wrote, " 'Doctor' John Brinkley, one of the nation's most successful quacks, was making a fortune by grafting goat glands to the testicles of aging men. Of course no goat gland was needed to provide virility for the Mighty Casey." *Annotated Casey*, p. 193.

14. *Baseball Magazine*, November 1925, p. 547.

15. *SN*, August 19, 1926.

16. *Baseball Magazine*, October 1929, p. 510.

17. Ibid., May 1937, p. 544.

Chapter 7: "Casey" Carries On

1. Gardner, *Annotated Casey*, p. 54.

2. Ibid., pp. 55, 57–58.

3. *SL*, November 24, 1906.

4. William F. Kirk, *Right Off the Bat: Baseball Ballads* (New York: G. W. Dillingham Co., 1911), pp. 17–18.

5. *SL*, January 17, 1914.

6. Ibid., July 18, 1914.

7. Ibid., January 23, 1915.

8. Ibid., February 13, 1915.

9. L. H. Baker, *Football: Facts and Figures* (New York: Farrar and Rinehart, Inc., 1945), pp. 155–58, 232.

10. *Baseball Magazine*, February 1917, p. 72.

11. Gardner, *Annotated Casey*, p. 78.

12. Ibid., pp. 79–80.

13. *Baseball Magazine*, January 1936, p. 364.

14. Ibid., November-December 1954, p. 16.

15. Ibid., June 1924, p. 319.

16. *Mad Magazine*, January 1969, pp. 19–21.

17. Gardner, *Annotated Casey*, pp. 161–63.

18. Ibid., pp. 155–57.

19. Gardner to author, April 6, 1972.

20. *SL*, July 24, 1909.

Chapter 8: The Family

1. Gardner, *Annotated Casey*, pp. 96–99.

2. *Baseball Magazine*, February 1911, pp. 71–72; Gardner, *Annotated Casey*, pp. 106–8.

3. William F. Kirk, *Right Off the Bat*, pp. 33–34.

4. *Baseball Magazine*, January 1911, pp. 61–62.

5. Gardner, *Annotated Casey*, pp. 103–4. In a remarkable coincidence, it appears that the name of Nitram Rendrag, when spelled backwards, is Martin Gardner.

6. Ibid., pp. 111–13; Robinson, "Casey's Daughter at the Bat," pp. 390–91. The poem was first published in Franklin P. Adams's column in the *New York Post*, June 29, 1939, and was included in Adams's anthology *Innocent Merriment* in 1942. Gardner, *Annotated Casey*, p. 110.

Chapter 9: Parodies

1. *SN*, March 1, 1902. In the original printing, the last word of the second line of the fourth stanza, was "bent," obviously an error.

2. *SL*, March 30, 1907.

3. *New York Times*, October 1, 1907.

4. *Detroit News Tribune*, October 6, 1907. This was the Sunday edition of the *Detroit News*.

5. See chapter three.

6. *Baseball Magazine*, August 1916, pp. 51–52.

7. *SN*, October 26, 1911.

8. *SL*, December 2, 1911. This ballad was reprinted in *Baseball Magazine*, May 1912, p. 52.

9. *Baseball Magazine*, January 1921, p. 368.

10. *SN*, January 30, 1921.

11. *Baseball Magazine*, December 1923, p. 297.

12. *Colliers*, October 6, 1928, p. 7.

13. *Baseball Magazine*, November 1925, p. 540. With reference to stanza two, line one, Ruth had a bad year in 1925.

14. Dave Camerer, ed., *The Best of Grantland Rice*, p. 139.

15. Gardner, *Annotated Casey*, pp. 167–69.

16. Dr. Tilden G. Edelstein of Rutgers recited this poem in the course of delivering a paper on the Cohen brothers—Andy and Sid—before the Organization of American Historians in Cincinnati in April 1983. The poem is from the "Andy Cohen Scrapbook" and is reprinted through the courtesy of Professor Edelstein.

17. *SN*, October 16, 1941.

18. Ibid., June 26, 1946.

19. Ibid., January 29, 1947. Written by Joseph Farrell, the poem was recited by the actor Walter Huston at a baseball banquet in Chicago, January 19, 1947.

20. Ibid., January 17, 1953.

21. The poem was reprinted in the *New York Times*, October 10, 1969.

22. *Congressional Record*, October 23, 1975.

23. *Pittsburgh Press*, April 11, 1976.

24. Undated Associated Press newsclipping. Of course, the Yankees won the series, four games to two.

25. Author's copy.

Chapter 10: Leftovers

1. Gardner, *Annotated Casey*, pp. 51–52.

2. *SL*, December 27, 1913. Pages 9 through 16 of this issue were dated December 20.

3. Ibid., May 11, 1912. At the end of the poem, Rice wrote, "Substitute Phillies, Yankees or seven or eight other big league clubs."

4. *Baseball Magazine*, April 1918, p. 490.

5. Jack Regan and Will E. Stahl, *On the Road With the Baseball Bugs* (Chicago: J. Regan and Co., 1910), pp. 74–75.

6. *SL*, July 24, 1909.

7. *SN*, July 1, 1915.

8. Ibid., July 19, 1923.

9. *SL*, September 26, 1908.

10. *Mad Magazine*, October 1960, pp. 70–72.

11. *Baseball Magazine*, August 1926, p. 390.

12. Gardner, *Annotated Casey*, p. 60.

13. Ibid., pp. 61–64.

Chapter 11: Grand Opera

1. Gardner, *Annotated Casey*, p. 12.

2. Ibid.

3. Ibid.

4. Robinson, "Casey's Daughter at the Bat," p. 390; Jeremy Gury to author, April 18, 1972.

5. William Schuman and Jeremy Gury, *The Mighty Casey* (New York: G. Schirmer, Inc., 1954), pp. 12–18. The opera was premiered in Hartford, Connecticut, in May 1953.

6. Ibid., pp. 42–44; Gardner, *Annotated Casey*, p. 178.

7. Schuman and Gury, *The Mighty Casey*, pp. v, 44–45. Since only nine players were listed on the Mudville roster, one has to be curious to know who replaced Flynn following his numerous "benchings." On another matter, the cosmopolitan makeup of the team, it might be observed, hardly comported with the Anglo-Saxon nationality composition of a typical American small town in the nineteenth century. However, this was the very point the authors wished to make: the Mudville team was intended to be representative of the country and all its people, both then and now. Ibid., p. v.

8. Ibid., pp. 21–24, 59–62.

9. Ibid., pp. 65, 69–108.

10. Ibid., pp. 109–35.

11. Ibid., pp. 149–56.

12. Ibid., pp. 158–62.

13. Gardner, *Annotated Casey*, p. 14; *Stockton Record*, July 12, 1955.

Chapter 12: Mighty Casey: All-American

1. From *God's Country and Mine*, quoted in Charles Einstein, ed., *The Second Fireside Book of Baseball* (New York: Simon and Schuster, 1958), p. 20. As a student in one of Barzun's classes at Columbia University in the late 1940s, I was impressed by his brilliance as a scholar, but that he was a follower of baseball and knew quite a bit about the game was a revelation.

2. Bruce Catton, "The Great American Game," *American Heritage* 10 (April 1959): 17.

3. William Patten and J. Walker McSpadden, *The Book of Baseball* (New York: P. F. Collier and Son, 1911), foreword; H. Addington Bruce, "Baseball and the National Life," *Outlook Magazine*, May 17, 1913, p. 104.

4. Richter, *History and Records*, p. 201; Elizabeth Nowell, ed., *The Letters of Thomas Wolfe* (New York: Charles Scribner's Sons, 1956), p. 722.

5. Lee Allen, *100 Years of Baseball* (New York: Bartholomew House, Inc., 1950), p. vi.

6. Roger Angell, "Baseball in the Mind," in *This Great Game* (Englewood Cliffs, N.J.: Prentice-Hall, 1971), pp. 26–27.

7. Schuman and Gury, *The Mighty Casey*, pp. v–vi; Catton, "The Great American Game," p. 17.

8. Art Hill, *Don't Let Baseball Die* (Au Train, Mich.: Avery Color Studios, 1978), p. vii.

9. Douglass Wallop, *Baseball: An Informal History* (New York: W. W. Norton and Co., Inc., 1969), p. 21.

10. James T. Farrell, *My Baseball Diary* (New York: A. S. Barnes and Co., 1957), pp. 39–40.

11. Coffin, *The Illustrated Book of Baseball Folklore*, pp. 46–63.

12. Anton Grobani, *Guide to Baseball Literature* (Detroit: Gale Research Co., 1975); Richter, *History and Records*, p. 201.

13. Ralph S. Graber, "Baseball in American Fiction," *English Journal* 56 (November 1967): 1108–1110.

14. Ibid., pp. 1111–1114.

15. Spalding, *America's National Game*, p. 449; Earl Schenk Miers, *Baseball* (New York: Grosset and Dunlap, 1967), p. 7.

16. Dr. Wishart received two "standing 'O's" from the student body after he had finished and retired to his chair. *Cleveland Plain Dealer*, October 10, 1941. After his recital I decided to memorize the poem and have "performed" it a number of times. Unfortunately, like Jerome Gury, I learned the corrupted version.

17. Gardner, *Annotated Casey*, pp. 14–15.

18. Coffin, *The Illustrated Book of Baseball Folklore*, pp. 127–33.

19. William Lyon Phelps, *What I Like in Poetry* (New York: Charles Scribner's Sons, 1934), p. 16.

20. *Cleveland Plain Dealer*, October 10, 1941.

Bibliography

Although "Casey at the Bat" has a long history and parodies and variations based on it are numerous, there is not an extensive literature on the subject. All the pertinent works have been mentioned in the notes. In this bibliography no attempt is made to list all the printings of "Casey at the Bat." However, a number of the most famous or most elaborate printings are mentioned. Also, since the sources for all the poems used in the book are cited in the notes they will not be repeated here.

A listing of the "Casey" literature must be prefaced by a few words about the pioneering research of Martin Gardner, which resulted in his *Annotated Casey at the Bat* in 1967. Gardner possesses an original and imaginative mind. His writings include several "annotated" collections, countless mathematical, scientific, and space puzzle books, as well as serious works in science, philosophy, and literature. A *New York Times* critic wrote that Gardner's *Flight of Peter Fromm* was a "brilliantly illuminating metaphysical novel that employs ideas as adversaries and translates them into human dilemmas."

One wonders how such a prolific writer as Martin Gardner found time to put together *The Annotated Casey*. Nevertheless, he spent many hours in research at the New York Public Library and the Baseball Hall of Fame in Cooperstown gathering materials which went into his book. Building upon a lifelong interest in baseball and a broad knowledge of literature, he composed a fresh and original volume about one of our folk heroes. Not that "Casey" would have been forgotten. But Gardner has given "Casey" a new stature and respectability. Without his work my own task would have been much more difficult than it was. Thus I view this book as an "extension" of *The Annotated Casey at the Bat*.

Books

Allen, Lee, *The Hot Stove League* (New York: A. S. Barnes and Co., 1955).
————, *100 Years of Baseball* (New York: Bartholomew House, Inc., 1950).
Bready, James, *The Home Team* (Washington, D.C.: published by author, 1971).
Camerer, Dave, ed., *The Best of Grantland Rice* (New York: Franklin Watts, Inc., 1963).
Claudy, C. H., *The Battle of Baseball* (New York: The Century Co., 1912).
Coffin, Tristram P., *The Old Ball Game: Baseball in Folklore and Fiction* (New York: Herder and Herder, 1971).

————, *The Illustrated Book of Baseball Folklore* (New York: Seabury Press, 1975).

Einstein, Charles, ed., *The Fireside Book of Baseball* (New York: Simon and Schuster, 1956).

————, *The Second Fireside Book of Baseball* (New York: Simon and Schuster, 1958).

————, *The Third Fireside Book of Baseball* (New York: Simon and Schuster, 1968).

Farrell, James T., *My Baseball Diary* (New York: A. S. Barnes and Co., 1957).

Felleman, Hazel, *Best Loved Poems of the American People* (Garden City, N.Y.: Doubleday and Co., 1936).

Gardner, Martin, *The Annotated Casey at the Bat* (New York: Clarkson N. Potter, Inc., 1967).

Grobani, Anton, *Guide to Baseball Literature* (Detroit: Gale Research Co., 1975).

Hill, Art, *Don't Let Baseball Die* (Au Train, Mich.: Avery Color Studios, 1978).

Hopper, De Wolf, with Stout, Wesley Winans, *Reminiscences of De Wolf Hopper: Once a Clown Always a Clown* (Garden City, N.Y.: Garden City Publishing Co., 1925).

Kennedy, Charles O'Brien, *American Ballads: Naughty, Ribald, and Classic* (New York: Fawcett Publications, paper, 1952).

————, *A Treasury of American Ballads, Gay, Naughty, and Classic* (New York: The McBride Co., 1954).

Kirk, William F., *Right Off the Bat: Baseball Ballads* (New York: G. W. Dillingham Co., 1911).

Knowles, Frederic Lawrence, *A Treasury of Humorous Poetry* (Boston: Dana, Estes and Co., 1902).

Miers, Earl Schenk, *Baseball* (New York: Grosset and Dunlap, 1967).

Nowell, Elizabeth, ed., *The Letters of Thomas Wolfe* (New York: Charles Scribner's Sons, 1956).

Palmer, Harry Clay, *Athletic Sports in America, England, and Australia* (Philadelphia: Hubbard Brothers, Publishers, 1889).

Patten, William, and McSpadden, J. Walker, *The Book of Baseball* (New York: P. F. Collier and Son, 1911).

Phelps, William Lyon, *What I Like in Poetry* (New York: Charles Scribner's Sons, 1934).

Regan, Jack, and Stahl, Will E., *On the Road with the Baseball Bugs* (Chicago: J. Regan and Co., Publishers, 1910).

Rice, Grantland, *Baseball Ballads* (Nashville: The Tennesseean Co., 1910).

————, *Only the Brave* (New York: A. S. Barnes and Co., 1941).

————, *The Tumult and the Shouting* (New York: A. S. Barnes and Co., 1954).

Richter, Francis C., *History and Records of Baseball* (Philadelphia: published by author, 1914).

Santayana, George, *Persons and Places* (New York: Charles Scribner's Sons, 1944).

Seymour, Harold, *Baseball: The Early Years* (New York: Oxford University Press, 1960).

————, *Baseball: The Golden Age* (New York: Oxford University Press, 1971).

Spalding, Albert G., *America's National Game* (New York: American Sports Publ. Co., 1911).

Spink, Alfred H., *The National Game* (St. Louis: National Publ. Co., 1911).

Stevenson, Burton E., *Famous Single Poems* (New York: Harcourt, Brace and Co., 1923; New York: Dodd, Mead and Co., 1935; Freeport, N.Y.: Books for Libraries Press, 1971).

————, *The Home Book of Verse* (New York: Henry Holt and Co., 1926).

Thayer, Ernest L., *Casey at the Bat* (New York: New Amsterdam Book Co., 1901; reprint Pasadena, Calif.: The Castle Press, 1977).

———, *Casey at the Bat*, ill. Paul Frame (Englewood Cliffs, N.J.: Prentice-Hall, 1964).

———, *Casey at the Bat*, ill. Jim Hull (New York: Dover Publications, 1977).

———, *Casey at the Bat*, ill. Wallace Tripp (New York: Coward, McCann, and Geoghegan, Inc., 1978).

Townsend, Doris, ed., *This Great Game* (Englewood Cliffs, N.J.: Prentice-Hall, 1971).

Voigt, David Q., *American Baseball: From Gentleman's Sport to the Commissioner System* (Norman, Okla.: University of Oklahoma Press, 1966).

———, *American Baseball: From the Commissioner System to Continental Expansion* (Norman, Okla.: University of Oklahoma Press, 1970).

Wallop, Douglass, *Baseball: An Informal History* (New York: W. W. Norton and Co., Inc., 1969).

Magazines and Journals

Austin, Anthony. "Seventy-Five Years Ago." *New York Times Magazine*, June 9, 1963, pp. 51, 54.

Berrigan, Darrell. "The Truth About Casey." *Saturday Evening Post*, July 3, 1954, pp. 30, 92–94.

Catton, Bruce. "The Great American Game." *American Heritage* 10 (April 1959): 16–25, 86.

Croy, Homer. "Casey at the Bat." *Baseball Magazine*, October 1908, pp. 10–12.

Dunlop, Richard. "Was This the Real Casey?" *Baseball Digest*, July 1959, pp. 41–42.

Ghio, Joanne Mary. "Stockton is Casey's Mudville." *Baseball Digest*, May 1960, pp. 92–94.

Glenister, John W. "Who Wrote 'Casey at the Bat'?" *Baseball Magazine*, June 1908, pp. 59–60.

Graber, Ralph S. "Baseball in American Fiction." *English Journal* 56 (November 1967): 1107–14.

Koppett, Leonard. "The Day 'Casey' First Appeared." *Baseball Digest*, February 1962, pp. 20–22.

Peck, Harry Thurston. "Who Wrote 'Casey at the Bat'?" *The Scrap Book*, December 1908, pp. 947–54.

Simard, Wesley. "Casey at the Bat." *Far Westerner*, July 1966, pp. 8–9.

Newspapers

All newspaper articles which were either used or consulted appeared in the following newspapers on the dates indicated.

Cleveland Leader: March 4, 1909.

Cleveland Plain Dealer: October 10, 1941.

New York Times: October 1, 1907; March 13, 1932; September 9, 14, 1958; March 8, 1970.

Portland Oregonian: June 28, 1909.

The Sporting News: November 9, 1901; January 28, 1905; January 20, 1906; October
     26, 1911; November 15, 29, 1923; May 23, 1935; December 3, 1936; March
     10, 17, 31, 1938; April 7, 1938; May 12, 1938; August 29, 1940; February 27,
     1941; June 5, 1941; February 18, 1943; June 10, 1953; September 2, 1953.
Stockton Independent: March 25, 1888; April 3, 1888; May 22, 1888.
Stockton Record: August 27, 29, 1952; December 30, 1952; June 4, 12, 1953; June 3,
     5, 7, 1954; June 11, 1955; July 12, 1955.

Reference and Special Works

Baseball Encyclopedia (New York: Macmillan, 1974).
Contemporary Authors (Detroit: Gale Research Co., 1978), vols. 73–76.
National Cyclopedia of American Biography (New York: 1947), vol. 33.
Something About the Author (Detroit: Gale Research Co., 1979), vol. 16.
Spalding Official Baseball Guide, 1884.

Opera

Schuman, William, and Gury, Jeremy, *The Mighty Casey* (New York: G. Schirmer,
     Inc., 1954).

Index

Recent Titles in
Contributions to the Study of Popular Culture

About the Author

EUGENE MURDOCK is Professor and Chairman of the Department of History at Marietta College. His earlier works include *Ban Johnson: Czar of Baseball* (Greenwood Press, 1982) and other books and articles on the Civil War and sports history.